THE CELEBRITY KOSHER COOKBOOK

A Sentimental Journey with Food, Mothers and Memories

BY MARILYN HALL AND RABBI JEROME CUTLER

Recipes tested by Ruth Jubelier Greenwold,
Lecturer, Gourmet Cooking, U.C.L.A. Extension

Published by
J.P. Tarcher, Inc., Los Angeles
Distributed by
Hawthorn Books, Inc., New York

The story by Rhoda Morgenstern is copyrighted by MTM Enterprises.

The recipe for Baked Stuffed Fish by David Reuben is reprinted by permission of Random House, Inc., from *The Save-Your-Life Diet* by David Reuben; Copyright © 1975 by La Prensa Enterprises, Inc.

The recipe for Pecan Rum Cakes by Dinah Shore is from *Someone's in the Kitchen with Dinah* (Doubleday), copyright © 1972 by Dinah Shore.

Copyright © 1975 by Marilyn Hall and Jerome Cutler

All rights reserved

Library of Congress Catalog Card Number: 75-17012

ISBN: 0-87477-042-4

Manufactured in the United States of America

Published by J.P. Tarcher, Inc.
9110 Sunset Boulevard
Los Angeles, California 90069

Published simultaneously in Canada by
Prentice-Hall of Canada, Ltd.
1870 Birchmount Road, Scarborough, Ontario

1 2 3 4 5 6 7 8 9 0

The royalties from the sale of this book go to the Synagogue for the Performing Arts of Los Angeles and to other Jewish charities across the country.

TABLE OF CONTENTS

INTRODUCTION/by Marilyn Hall

We reached them with our requests by letters, some of which languished in their accumulative mail for weeks while they were on tour, or making a film. We called them on the telephone, frustrating messages transmitted from one answering service to another, sluiced through secretaries and public relations men, missed and finally answered after weekends in Palm Springs or Vegas and bouts of the flu.

Many were buttonholed at social events, hearing but not wanting to hear the request, some responding graciously, others tolerantly, acknowledging the obligations of friendship. Their replies frequently came in fragmented, off the cuff, ad lib. But all gave us a slice of their lives and with it a moment of very personal history.

Their mothers and grandmothers come through in vivid glimpses—the newcomers to this land, clutching their culture like a warm comforter—finding solace in the kitchen at the stove—chopping, mixing, beating—expressing in every meal the symbiotic relationship between food and love that is a triumph of Jewish psychology.

For some this heritage became fragmented, diluted through a new national identity. And as success came, the mothers who had paid their dues in the early years found a new freedom; and it was not unfrequent that their kosher kitchens took on a distinctive Southern, Jamaican or Mexican accent as surrogate cooks took over at the stove.

As the children left the enclave and became aware of a larger world, most shed their parochial skins and every time they came home from a new triumph, the kitchen seemed smaller than they had remembered it. Often they brought back strangers to their Jewish home, and this exchange of cultures caused many amusing incidents which they reveal with relish, such as the time the new non-Jewish wife of an actor went into a delicatessen, and not being very hungry, ordered bagels, cream cheese—and one lock. Memories are kept alive by retelling and for many our request was a reawakening of times past and as though they were waiting for the cue, a rush of words spilled out. Others refused the prod and chose to go a contemporary way—telling a "now" story.

How close these families were—whether out of love or a sense of duty and respect. If one of the grandparents died, they closed ranks and somehow the roof covered them all, or a move was made and the new apartment nestled nearer the central home. There was no thought of exile.

From the recipes, it appeared that Jewish life centered around brisket, noodle pudding and fried matzo. Brisket was an expensive cut of meat, but it was an indulgence that helped to sanctify the sabbath. There was an emphasis on sweet and sour dishes, like a symbol of their lives—fraught with moments of joy and moments of sadness. The tradition of handling down recipes from one generation to another was sometimes hard to decipher. The older generation never wrote anything down—it was a relay of information to be decanted and demystified by the new bride of the family. "Baba, how do you make strudel?" asked a young girl. "It's easy, mein kind. First I wash my hands. Then I put a net on my hair." "And then, Baba?" "And then—I make strudel!"

And so this book is a nod toward things that were and things that are. Sometimes as these personalities jet through the skies and catch the anxious look on an older lady's face, they start to fantasize, and the "Coffee, tea or milk?" they hear is translated into "Eat, my child; it's good for you." Looking back on their lives, they realize—it was just their way.

KASHRUT/by Rabbi Jerome Cutler

The laws of Kashrut (keeping Kosher) are found in various books of the Bible. No explanations are given. It is the duty of the Jew to follow the word of God, regardless of His inte..t or meaning. In retrospect we can see that there were many health reasons attached to the commandments of forbidden food; however, in the observant Jew's adherence to the law, the health aspect was secondary. The observance of God's commandment was—and is—his primary concern.

Man, it seems, was originally intended to be a vegetarian. In Genesis 1:29, God said, "See, I give you every seed-bearing plant that is upon the earth and every tree that has seed-bearing plant; they shall be yours for food." But as all things evolve through the process of time, so did man's eating habits, and eating meat became an integral part of human behavior.

Not all meat, however, was permitted. Although the book of Leviticus (11:3) states, "Whatsoever parteth the hoof and is wholly cloven-footed and cheweth the cud among the beasts, that ye may eat," it thereby eliminated many animals that didn't fall in such categories. As for fish, Leviticus (11:9) says, "These may ye eat of all that are in the waters; whatsoever hath fins and scales." Thus, shellfish, frogs, whales, porpoises, dolphins, etc., are prohibited.

Also not allowed are combined meat and dairy dishes, as it is written "You shall not boil a kid in its mother's milk"— Exodus (23:19, 34:26, Deuteronomy 14:21). The reason this commandment appears three times is due to the basic cruelty involved in combining the milk, the life-giving element of an animal, with the element of death, its flesh.

Now that we have explained on one foot what is edible according to dietary laws, one still cannot run out to the local A & P and buy a chicken and claim that since it falls into the realm of permissible foods, it is kosher. Kosher means properly prepared or "ritually proper." Chances are the A & P chicken had not been killed according to the practice of "shehita" (ritual slaughter). Meat falling under that category can be found at your friendly kosher meat market or in the frozen food counter of your local market in the proper packaging. The reason for the "shehita" is so that we know the meat was slaughtered by a shohet, one who is specifically trained and authorized to perform shehita, and has not been killed in any other way or died a natural death.

Many Jews observe "Biblical Kashrut" only. They do not eat the flesh of animals or fish prohibited by the Torah and they do not mix meat and dairy together, but they also do not observe the laws of shehita.

Many more no longer adhere to the tenets of Kashrut at all. First and foremost, it's easier not to. Secondly, with the government so closely watching over hygienic conditions in restaurants and over the slaughter of meat and the packaging of food, there is no longer the threat of trichinosis in pork or harmful germs in shellfish.

The modern Jew, however, who observes the ritual today does so because there is a spiritual and ethical lesson in Kashrut. By curbing one's appetite for forbidden foods, even though they are tasty and not harmful, one learns to curb his appetite in all areas of life and to live moderately and purely. The Jew who keeps Kashrut has to think of his religious and communal allegiance on the occasion of every meal; and on every such occasion the observance of those laws constitutes a renewal of acquiescence in the fact of his culture and heritage.

COMMENTS FROM THE TEST KITCHEN/by Ruth Jubelier Greenwold

Over one hundred recipes to test. All from Master Chefs, for whose mother made the soul food of one's youth anything less than perfect?

We have taken tiny liberties with some of the recipes, for how else could the rest of us try to duplicate these delicacies without common denominators—the basic guidelines for measurements, procedures, cooking terms? We have no nostalgic memory of *that* kitchen, *that* mother using deft fingers and equipment peculiar to her: that earless cup, still too useful to be discarded—did it hold 5 or 5¼ ounces? And how much more was "heaping"? Was the designated spoonful a soup spoon, a dessert spoon or a teaspoon? Were these the large European spoons from her dowry, or the less ample New World spoons? How much is a handful? How big the cupped hand?

So, as you see, it was imperative to translate recipes into a standard language so that those of us who can't dream back to the particular kitchen and special Master Chef will have a fighting chance to duplicate every delicious contribution to this book.

The only measure that can't be standardized is the full measure of love that I am sure went into the execution of these dishes each time they were produced. So, I urge you to add the same ingredient. It is the one magic item that makes everything successful and that withstands the test of time.

Being Sure It's Kosher

When buying margarine, be sure that it is pareve and, therefore, usable with dairy dishes and even meat products. When buying any other dairy substitute, be sure that it is 100 percent milk free. All prepackaged products used in these recipes that contain shortening as an ingredient should stipulate vegetable shortening on the package.

Measures

All measures given in these recipes are with standard measuring cups and spoons.

1 cup = 8 liquid ounces = 16 tablespoons.
2 cups = 1 pint = 16 ounces.
4 cups = 1 quart = 32 ounces.
1 tablespoon = 3 teaspoons = ½ ounce.
Pinch = the amount you can hold between your thumb and forefinger.

1 cube of butter or margarine $=$ ½ cup and weighs 4 ounces.

Standard Cooking Terms

Boil—to create a churning, restless sea of ever-breaking bubbles in your pot containing liquid (this requires high heat); you can boil at lower heat so that your water bubbles less actively—but bubbles.

Simmer—first you bring your liquid to the active bubbling stage, then reduce the heat till the surface of the liquid barely breaks with lazy bubbles.

Poach—the liquid is just at the boil; the surface just quivers gently, but no bubbles break.

Saute—to brown or cook food in fat in an uncovered pan.

Stir—to keep food or sauce moving with a spoon, spatula or whisk.

Beat—stir vigorously.

Fold—to combine gently (this is done with egg whites that have been beaten into clouds); a rubber spatula is a good utensil for this.

Knead—to work a flour mixture until it is smooth and elastic (the equipment—your hands).

Grate—to reduce to shreds or juice with a grater.

Roast—to cook meat or fowl uncovered in the oven, using a rack and *no* liquid.

Stew (gedempt)—to cook meat using liquid to tenderize; this may be done in the oven or on top of the stove; the pot is covered.

Blessed art Thou,
O Lord Our God,
King of the Universe,
Who Brings forth food from the earth.

APPETIZERS

KEN HOLTZMAN • Anchovy and Egg Appetizer
GEORGE JESSEL • Kosher Caviar
                   • Chicken Liver Pate
JACK KRUSCHEN • Poor Man's Caviar
LEONARD NIMOY • Pickled Herring
CARL REINER • Roumanian Potlegele (Eggplant)

KEN HOLTZMAN/Anchovy and Egg Appetizers

St. Louis Blues

I was born in St. Louis. My grandparents, who came from Russia, kept a kosher house and we always went there on Friday nights and for seders.

I went to Hebrew school and was bar mitzvahed, but my interest in sports interfered with my studies. One of the Hebrew schools was right across the street from a park, and the sound of the crack of the bat was a terrible distraction. Sometimes I would skip school or sneak out a little early to go over and play baseball.

My wife and I keep a kosher home, but it's hard to stay kosher when you travel a lot. Once I made special arrangements with an airline so I could be served a kosher meal during the flight. It turned out to be pork chops! I couldn't even eat the bread because they didn't serve the butter. At least they were half right. Unfortunately, El Al does not fly to most American League Cities.

Anchovy and Egg Appetizers • Serves 6-8

1 tin anchovies, cut into slivers (leave one or two strips of anchovy whole to decorate top of eggs)
6 hard-cooked eggs, chopped or grated coarsely
2-3 tablespoons mayonnaise
1 tablespoon lemon juice (to taste)
Salt and pepper to taste
2-3 tablespoons sour cream
Chopped fresh dill or parsley
3 scallions

Method: Combine the chopped egg and slivers of anchovy and chopped scallions. Moisten with mayonnaise. Season to taste with lemon juice, salt and pepper. Arrange in a mound in a pretty dish or in a cupped lettuce leaf. Spread sour cream over top of mound. Decorate with the whole anchovy strips and sprinkle with fresh dill or parsley.

Serve with crackers or thinly sliced pumpernickel or rye.

GEORGE JESSEL/Kosher Caviar & Chicken Liver Pate

Miami Memories

I'm the inventor of the Bloody Mary.

It happened in a hotel in Miami, Florida in 1931. You may remember I was married to Norma Talmadge, and her sister was Constance Talmadge. When Constance drank a good deal in the evening, she'd have a hangover in the morning and would ask for "anything with tomato juice and booze." One morning when I was down in the hotel bar mixing up a "tomato juice and booze" for her, the bartender said to me, "Here's a bottle, Mr. Jessel, that's been here for seven years. No one's ever asked for it. It's called 'voodkey.'" (In those days most people didn't even know how to say "vodka.") So I took it, mixed the vodka with the juice and, with a bit of inspiration, added a little lemon and Worcestershire in it. First I called it "Good Morning, Charlie," and then "Fun Behind the Bar."

One day after a night of dissipation, a rich Philadelphia playgirl named Mary came into the bar and asked for a morning cap. "Try this," I said, and handed her my concoction. A little under the weather, she spilt it on her gown, and so that morning I called it "Bloody Mary."

Six months later every bar in Florida had it, and the first thing you know, Smirnoff had it, too, and they took a couple of ads with me, and there you are. The rest is history.

I would much rather have invented the Singer sewing machine.

Kosher Caviar
• Serves 4-6

1 cup roe (can be obtained at Jewish fish market)
2 teaspoons vinegar
2 cups water
1 teaspoon salt
2-3 teaspoons salt
2-3 tablespoons mayonnaise
2 tablespoons chopped stuffed olives or pickles
   or
Lemon juice and onion juice to taste

Method: Cook roe 10 to 15 minutes in 2 cups of water that has been acidified with 2 teaspoons vinegar and 1 teaspoon salt. Drain cooked roe, plunge into cold water and drain again. Remove membrane that encloses roe. Separate roe eggs. Mash roe up with 2 to 3 teaspoons salt. Mix well. Allow to marinate in refrigerator for a day or longer. Combine salted roe, mayonnaise and chopped pickles or olives. Or, combine salted roe with lemon and onion juice to taste before serving.

Chicken Liver Pate
• Serves 6-8

1 pound chicken livers
3 tablespoons chicken fat
1 or 2 onions, chopped
2 hard-cooked eggs
    Salt and pepper to taste
    Mustard or celery salt (optional)
    Garnish (optional): chicken fat, grated
    hard-cooked egg

Method: Saute chicken livers in 2 tablespoons chicken fat till livers change color and are just done. Remove from pan. Add another tablespoon chicken fat and saute onions till they are gold-tinged. Chop livers, onions and hard-cooked eggs very fine. *Or,* put through food mill to make a very smooth pate. Season with salt, pepper to taste. Add mustard or celery salt if desired.

Some people like to decorate top of pate mound with a tablespoon of partially set chicken fat. A hard-cooked egg, grated, may also decorate the pate.

JACK KRUSCHEN/Poor Man's Caviar

This Story Is for the Birds

My father, who was in the Russian Army when the revolution started, went over the hill to Turkey and sent for my mother. Evenutally they moved to Winnipeg, where I was born.

When my mother and father first got married, she didn't know how to cook at all. She had worked with her sister as a milliner and they made marvelous dramatic hats for the Czar's family and many people of the court. Their specialties were creations that simulated stuffed birds.

For my parents' first meal, my mother bought a chicken. She chopped off the head and feet (in those days you bought a chicken complete with all the noise) and put in all the seasonings she seemed to remember her mother doing. When my father came into the house for dinner, a strange, acrid odor assaulted him. In front of him on the plate lay a poor unfortunate bird with marcelled feathers. Stunned, my father stared at the bird and then burst into laughter. "A bird of paradise for a hat you know how to stuff, but a bird to eat . . .!"

Poor Man's Caviar   • Serves 8-10

1 medium to large eggplant
1 large firm tomato, blanched by dipping in boiling water for a minute, then in cold water, then peeled
1 medium onion (red or white), peeled and diced
½ pound Greek olives (black), pitted
1 clove garlic, finely chopped (optional)
½ cup olive oil, or less, to taste
¾ cup wine vinegar, or to taste
Salt and pepper to taste

Method: Wash eggplant. Place on pie pan or similar container in 375-degree oven. Bake 45 minutes or until soft to the touch. Allow to cool and then peel and chop with the peeled tomato, diced onion, pitted olives, and clove of garlic (if used). Chop till mixture is well combined and fine. Add oil and vinegar, salt and pepper to taste. Allow to marinate in refrigerator overnight.

Serve with rye bread and/or pumpernickel slices.

5

LEONARD NIMOY/Pickled Herring

The Secret Ingredients

I grew up in Boston. My grandparents lived in the apartment with us, and our whole family life centered around the kitchen. As soon as you walked into the house, there was a meal on the table, you sat down and talked and ate. When one meal was finished, the next was in preparation.

My grandmother taught my mother to cook, and my mother taught me this pickled herring. When she came out to California, I watched her make it and took careful notes. Then I made it myself, using the exact measurements I had recorded. But it didn't work perfectly for me. Finally I came to the conclusion that the missing ingredient was my mother's touch. However, everybody loved my herring—especially my mother. She felt that hers had always been good but what it needed was *my* touch.

Pickled Herring • Serves 3-4

2 schmaltz herring
2 onions, sliced
1 cup vinegar
½ cup water
3 or more tablespoons sugar, to taste
1 cup sour cream
1 tablespoon whole pickling spice (optional)

Method: Soak herring whole overnight. Remove skins and entrails. Filet herring and cut into pieces; or cut into slices through bone. Place herring in jar in layers alternating with the sliced onions. Combine vinegar, water, sugar and sour cream. Pour over herring. Store in refrigerator for a day or two before serving.

If you like it sweeter, add more sugar; sour, add vinegar. If you wish, omit sour cream in the pickling liquid. Instead, add it to the drained, pickled herring when ready to serve. A tablespoon of whole pickling spice added to the marinade adds zest.

CARL REINER/Roumanian Potlegele (Eggplant)

The Quest

My mother used to make a big batch of potato latkes every Sunday. They'd turn out nice and crispy and brown, but my brother didn't like them.

It seems that one time when he was very young, there were a lot of latkes left over from lunch and they were put on a plate on the steam radiator to hold till dinner. (I can still hear them crackle on the plate.) Of course, the potatoes turned green. My brother had the leftover latkes for the evening meal and loved them. From then on, he wouldn't eat them until they turned green. Then I also got to thinking—because he was my older brother and knew best—that green potato latkes were perfect. So I stopped eating potato latkes in the afternoon and waited until the evening meal when they were moss green. To this day I'm still looking for green potato latkes. But now there's forced air heat, there are no steam radiators, and the green potato latke is no longer with us. It is a vestige of early Bronx apartments.

Roumanian Potlegele (Eggplant)

1 eggplant, dark purple and firm
Lemon juice
Salt
2 tablespoons salad oil
⅓ medium onion, finely diced

Method: Insert long-handled fork under stem of eggplant and place eggplant on gas jet turned high. Turn eggplant over once or twice until it is fully cooked. (To test, prick skin; if steam comes out, it is done.) Put eggplant under cold running tap. Peel off charred skin. Remove top and place eggplant in a bowl. Squeeze lemon juice over it. Tilt platter to drain off bitter eggplant juice. Chop with wooden spoon to soften. Sprinkle liberally with salt, more lemon juice and salad oil. Put in covered jar and store in refrigerator for a week to marinate. When ready to use, mix with diced onion. May be used as an hors d'oeuvre, spread on crackers, cucumber slices, etc.

If used as salad, it will serve 3-4. As a hors d'oeuvre, it should serve 6-8.

SOUPS AND ACCOMPANIMENTS

ED AMES • Przepalanka (Potato Soup)
RICHARD BENJAMIN • Chilled Almond Bisque
ABE BURROWS • Dutch Pea Soup and Meatballs
RED BUTTONS • Puerto Rican Farfel Soup
BILL MACY • Chicken Soup
SOUPY SALES • Milchig Fish Soup
WILLIAM SHATNER • Matzo Kneidlach (Passover
Dumplings)
ABIGAIL (DEAR ABBY) VAN BUREN • Cucumber
Vichyssoise

ED AMES/Przepalanka

Saturday Afternoons

I had to learn Yiddish to speak to my grandmother, whom I visited once a week. At the time I thought she felt it was a duty call on my part; but just before she died, she gave me a beautiful prayer book, and I realized how much my visits really meant to her. I have that book to this day and often open it and read a passage and remember my grandmother.

I remember many other things about my boyhood in Boston, particularly those wonderful, cozy Saturday afternoons when my mother would take out the ingredients to bake sugar cookies. We'd turn on the radio, and the dulcet tones of Milton Cross and the Metropolitan Opera would fill the room.

We'd listen to the great operas, and the smell of warm, sweet cookies permeated the room. Afterwards, we'd have them with tea, and my brothers and I would sing, accompanied by my mother, who played the guitar. I used to sing for my cookies; now I sing for my supper.

Przepalanka (Potato Soup) • Serves 6

4-6 potatoes, cut into small pieces
2 quarts water
2-3 tablespoons margarine, butter or other fat
2 tablespoons flour
  Salt and pepper to taste

Method: Cook potatoes in the 2 quarts of water till the potatoes are tender. Make a roux by melting the butter or other fat in a frying pan. Add flour, combine, cook and stir, using low heat till flour is golden. Remove from heat. Add some of the hot potato water to the roux. (Be careful. It will splatter at first.) Continue stirring as you do this till you make a smooth, creamy sauce. Add this to the potato mixture. Simmer for 10 or 15 minutes longer. Stir occasionally. Season to taste with salt and pepper.

If you use margarine or other fat, you can make this a fleishedike soup by adding slices of kosher frankfurters. Allow one frankfurter per person.

RICHARD BENJAMIN/Chilled Almond Bisque

Made to Order

Paula and I were on the *Queen Elizabeth*—the old one—and we ate in the fabulous Veranda Grill on the top of the ship where you have to have a special reservation. They prided themselves on doing something special for every guest. Anything you could think of, no matter how extraordinary or demanding, they would make for you. I wanted chopped liver. They said, "Well, how do you make it? Just give us an idea." I said, "Okay. It's chopped chicken livers, chopped egg, chopped sauteed onions and chicken fat." (I decided to forget the griebens.) And they said, "Fine, wonderful; we'll do that."

The next night they had it for me—all beautifully laid out—but in separate bowls: chopped liver, chopped egg, perfectly chopped up onion, and in a little French butter pat, the chicken fat. They presented it and said, "We hope this meets with your approval." I didn't have the heart. I said, "That's perfect."

Chilled Almond Bisque
• Serves 6

½ pound blanched almonds, ground very fine (set aside ¼ cup of almonds for topping)
½ cup milk
2 tablespoons butter
2 tablespoons flour
3 cups milk
Salt and pepper, to taste; pinch sugar
½ pint whipping cream, whipped

Method: Soak finely ground almonds one-half hour in ½ cup milk. Melt butter, add flour and stir 1 minute without browning. Slowly add 3 cups milk, stirring constantly. Cook and stir till mixture thickens. Add milk and soaked ground almonds, salt, pepper and pinch sugar. Cook 5 minutes longer. Correct seasoning. Remove from heat and chill in refrigerator. When ready to serve, whip cream. Fold about ½ of whipped cream into soup. Put a dollop of remaining whipped cream on top of each bowl of soup. Sprinkle with sliced, toasted almonds.

To toast almonds, place in a pie pan in 200-degree oven for 20 to 30 minutes. Let cool.

ABE BURROWS/Dutch Pea Soup and Meatballs

Just for Openers

My wife and I went to a kosher restaurant recently in New York and my wife asked for a demitasse.

The waiter brought the coffee in a large cup. My wife said, "Waiter, I ordered a demitasse."

The waiter, unflinching, said, "So, drink just a little."

If you go into a kosher restaurant, the best dishes are the openers—chopped liver, derma, lungen stew, pickled herring, and so on. The main dishes are not usually good. The chicken soup is always good, but by the time the same chicken is broiled or roasted as a main dish, it's already dried out and has lost its flavor. This wisdom, which took me many years to acquire, you now have in one short paragraph.

Dutch Pea Soup and Meatballs • Serves 4

½ **pound ground beef**
½ **teaspoon salt**
1 **teaspoon instant minced onion**
2 **envelopes Lipton's Pea Soup mix, prepared according to package instructions**
¼ **teaspoon ginger, to taste**

Method: Mix together beef, salt and instant onion. Form into balls the size of marbles. Prepare soup, stir in ginger and add meatballs. Simmer ¾ hour.

RED BUTTONS/Puerto Rican Farfel Soup

Se Habla Yiddish

I was very lucky. My grandmother was a great cook, my mother was a great cook. We came from a long line of great cooks. Nothing to eat, but a long line of great cooks. My wife Alicia is a great Puerto Rican cook, and she combines the two types of cooking with great success. There is very little difference between Jewish farfel soup and Puerto Rican farfel soup—maybe one year of high school. Puerto Rican farfel soup should never be eaten on Friday night unless you want to cha-cha-cha all through the Sabbath.

Puerto Rican Farfel Soup   • Serves 6-8

2½ quarts chicken broth (**canned, if desired**)
½ teaspoon green taco sauce
1 8-ounce can tomato sauce
2 cloves garlic, mashed
¼ teaspoon paprika
¼ teaspoon cilantro
1 onion, diced
  Salt to taste
2 stalks celery, diced
2 large potatoes, diced
½ package (8 ounces) farfel
  Parsley

Method: Add to chicken broth: taco sauce, tomato sauce, garlic, paprika, parsley, cilantro, onion, celery, salt. Cook 15 minutes to combine flavors. Add potatoes and farfel; cook 20 minutes more till potatoes and farfel are tender. Correct seasonings.

BILL MACY/Chicken Soup

Order It Again, Sam!

I grew up at Second Avenue and Eighth Street in New York. One day I introduced my non-Jewish wife to the B&H Dairy Restaurant on Second Avenue. She wanted to show me she was with it, so she ordered eggs and kasha. The waiter looked at her and asked, "So what kind of bread?" Samantha sweetly said, "I want kasha, please." The waiter didn't move. "So what kind of bread?" "Kasha," Samantha said. "Bread," the waiter retorted. "Kasha." "Bread." It was now becoming a "kasha and bread" tennis match. Finally, Samantha asserted herself. "Look, I don't want bread. I want kasha."

The waiter, defeated, shrugged his shoulders and went into the kitchen. After a few minutes he returned with a plate of eggs and kasha. Samantha gasped. "What is that?" she asked politely. "That's kasha!" "What happened to it?" "Nothing. But I think something happened to you!" "Isn't kasha the long, flat cracker?" "Kasha!" said the waiter in total disbelief. "You mean matzo!" She hasn't been able to live that down to this day.

Chicken Soup

1 fryer (a stewing hen will give better flavor but takes longer to cook)
   Cold water to cover chicken (about 2 quarts)
1 tablespoon salt
1 onion
2 carrots, unpeeled
1 stalk celery (green top, too)
2 or 3 baby parsnips
2 or 3 sprigs of parsley root from the tops (if you can get the parsley root or petrishke)

Method: Wash chicken, cut into pieces if desired and put into a 4-quart pot. Add water to about 1½ inches above chicken. Add salt, onion, carrots, celery and parsnips. Bring liquid to boil. Skim top. Reduce heat to simmer. Cover pot and cook about one hour till chicken is almost tender. Add parsley greens. Cook 15 to 20 minutes longer. Strain. Discard vegetables.

Serve soup either as a clear broth or with the chicken pieces in the soup.

SOUPY SALES/Milchig Fish Soup

Welcome to West Virginia

It was a ritual every year for my mother to make hamantaschen, and she made it like nobody else in the world—like little stars and triangles filled with prunes and poppyseed. We moved to a new home in Huntington, West Virginia, where the neighbors were really nice white bread people. My mother made a batch of hamantaschen, and as a friendly gesture, said, "I think I'll send some next door because they have a couple of kids." I took some over. The next day the little eight-year-old girl from next door came to our house and said, "Mrs. Baker, we want to thank you for sending that over." My mother replied, "Well, how did you like it?" The little girl hesitated. Then she answered, "It was really very interesting. We never had anything made with coffee grounds before."

One of my brothers was a serious eater. At the dinner table he was always saying, "What are we having for dinner next Wednesday?" And my mother would say, "You haven't eaten what you have today. Finish that and we'll talk about next Wednesday." He could never get enough dessert.

He was always trying to buy everybody's dessert. Strawberry shortcake was his special favorite. So one day my mother baked him a huge shortcake all his own and wouldn't let the rest of us touch it. My brother was delighted. His wildest fantasies were being realized. He ate more than half of it and suddenly stopped eating. To this day he pales visibly at the sight of a strawberry.

Milchig Fish Soup • Serves 4

2 onions, cut up
2 potatoes, cut up
1½ cups water
1 pound firm, white-fleshed fish, cut into pieces
3 tablespoons butter or margarine
1 cup milk
   Salt and pepper to taste

Method: Cook onion and potatoes in the water till potatoes are almost tender. Season with salt and pepper. Add the fish and cook 5 minutes, until fish flakes. Add milk, butter or margarine. Heat just to the boil, and serve.

WILLIAM SHATNER/Matzo Kneidlach (Passover Dumplings)

The Initiation

The first time I ever ate horseradish was during a Jewish holiday in Montreal. I was five or six at the time, and until then I hadn't been fed anything but bland baby food. But the time had come to prove my manhood.

I was given a small portion of the red, mushy substance but took too much on my fork. My eyes welled with tears, my face flushed, my nose ran, my ears burned. It was the Queen's Coronation, Fourth of July and Simchas Torah, all rolled into one.

Eating horseradish is like the Chinese recipe for curing aches and pains: beat your head against a wall, and the pain in your body goes away, and all that remains is the pain in your head. If you eat enough horseradish, nothing matters in the world, except the explosion in the center of your head.

My grandmother was a good cook who made the traditional Jewish dishes. Her favorite was kneidel. Not the soft, fluffy kneidel we know today, but a tightly packed, indestructible and delicious kneidel. To prevent rising beyond your station, she put a kneidel in your stomach. It made it very difficult to rise at all.

Matzo Kneidlach (Passover Dumplings)

2 eggs, separated
3 tablespoons chicken fat
½ cup hot water or hot parve broth
¼ cup matzo meal
½ teaspoon salt
2 quarts boiling broth or boiling salted water

Method: Beat egg yolks with chicken fat until thick and well blended. Pour over the hot water or hot broth and beat well. Add matzo meal mixed with the salt and then fold in egg whites that have been beaten until stiff but not dry. Chill for about 30 minutes. Wet hands with cold water and shape into small balls. Drop gently into two quarts boiling broth or boiling salted water. Reduce heat, cover and cook gently 20 to 25 minutes. Makes about 18.

ABIGAIL (Dear Abby) VAN BUREN/Cucumber Vichyssoise

Mama's Turkey Trot

My late beloved mother had four daughters (no sons). Even after we were married and had families, she invited us to her home for the traditional Thanksgiving dinner.

Mama insisted on doing everything herself. (And nobody was allowed to bring anything for the dinner either.)

I telephoned Mama around 9:30 Thanksgiving morning. "Hello, Mama," I said. "What are you doing?"

In that sweet sarcastic tone so typical of Jewish mothers, she replied, "What am I doing? . . . I'm dencing!" (She said it like that with her dialect.)

"Are you alone, Mama?" I asked solicitously.

"No . . .," she replied, "I've got en orchestra!"

Somehow, between numbers, she managed to get those Thanksgiving feasts and thousands of other meals on our table.

Cucumber Vichyssoise • Serves 6-8

3 medium-sized cucumbers (do not peel)
1 quart heavy sour cream
    Cold water to thin to desired consistency (about ¾ cup)
2 tablespoons Spice Island dill weed or finely chopped fresh dill weed.
    Salt and pepper to taste
2 tablespoons finely minced green onions (optional)

Method: Grate cucumbers, skin and all, by hand (do not put in a blender!), using coarsest side of old-fashioned type of four-sided grater. (Watch your knuckles!) Stir in sour cream. Stir in cold water to desired consistency. Add salt, pepper, onions and dill weed. Chill for several hours. Serve in chilled bowls. To garnish, a sprig of fresh parsley or an additional touch of dill weed can be added to each cup before serving.

SALADS AND SALAD DRESSINGS

ED ASNER • Ambrosia
BILL DANA • Greek Olive and Herring Salad
RODNEY DANGERFIELD • Soup Chicken Salad
BURT PRELUTSKY • Fiesta Salad
JOAN RIVERS • Pears and Caviar
NEIL SIMON • Cole Slaw
PETER YARROW • "You Are What You Eat" Salad
Dressing

ED ASNER/Ambrosia

Grade A Mom in a Grade B Movie

Dinner at my house was like a Grade B movie, the ones that had the ominous sound of bongo drums pounding incessantly and girls in grass skirts shimmying like my sister Kate—if I had one.

Picture, if you will, my beautiful Jewish mother. Slowly and regally she brings the food to us.

"Eat," she urges us, "eat."

She then waits patiently. After we finish eating, she collects the plates and eats what's left over.

In a way, in this beautiful princess' court, we were her tasters. And, she didn't even care if there was nothing left for her.

No, she wasn't an outstanding cook, but she was an outstanding mother.

Ambrosia

• Serves 6-8

1 cup sour cream
1 cup shredded coconut
1 cup white seedless grapes,
  or
1 cup diced or chunk pineapple, drained
1 cup diced walnuts
1 cup miniature marshmallows

Method: Mix all ingredients together and chill for several hours.

BILL DANA/Greek Olive and Herring Salad

Mother Knows Best

When I first made it big in show business, I wanted to show off my fancy home to my mother. It was a sprawling Mediterranean house with a wild gourmet kitchen that had everything—an electric blender, electric toaster, electric coffeemaker, electric microwave oven, electric everything.

Anxiously I showed my mother around to whet her appetite and then, the piece de resistance, the electric kitchen.

"What do you think, Ma?"

"That's very nice," she said.

The next day I got a big box with a lot of Manischewitz canned goods and a manually operated can opener. Inside I found a note. It said, "In case, darling, you should blow a fuse."

Greek Olive and Herring Salad

• Serves 6 for lunch

1 can matjes herring fillets (5½ ounces), bite size
1 large sweet onion, sliced thinly and separated into rings
¼ pound Greek olives (maslines)
1 small head cabbage, finely shredded
1 large green pepper, seeded and sliced into thin rings
2 or 3 tomatoes, diced or cut into eighths.
3 tablespoons olive oil
2 tablespoons wine vinegar or lemon juice to taste
    Salt and fresh ground pepper to taste
½ teaspoon powdered sugar (optional)

Method: Combine matjes herring, onion slices, Greek olives, shredded cabbage, green pepper rings and diced tomatoes. Toss with olive oil, wine vinegar or lemon juice. Season with salt, pepper and powdered sugar (if used). Allow to marinate in refrigerator for several hours. Toss a few times while marinating.

RODNEY DANGERFIELD/Soup Chicken Salad

No Respect

The other day my wife started up with me again. She told me she's tired, she's bored. She wants a new hobby.

I told her, "Why don't you take up cooking?"

She said to me, "When is the last time you thought of taking me out to dinner?"

I told her, "It was right after the last meal you cooked at home!"

I went shopping to a supermarket with her. She took the top off a container of sour cream to see if it was fresh. The sour cream was fresh but she still wouldn't take it. It was opened already.

Last time my wife fixed chicken, I got the wishbone. And if it works, that'll be her last chicken!

Soup Chicken Salad • Serves 4-6

2 or 3 cups cooked chicken, cut into bite-size pieces (skin and bone the cooked soup chicken and cut up)
½ cup walnut meats
3 stalks celery, cut into slices
1 cup seedless grapes (fresh if possible, or canned may be used)
1 green pepper, diced
¼ cup stuffed green olives, sliced
½ cup mayonnaise combined with ½ cup sour cream substitute
Lemon juice, salt, pepper to taste
Curry (optional) to taste
Mint or watercress garnish

Method: Combine all ingredients except mayonnaise mixture and seasonings. Moisten to taste with the mayonnaise mixture. Season with salt, pepper, lemon juice and curry (if used).

Serve on a bed of lettuce with watermelon chunks, fresh pineapple, etc., and decorate with mint or watercress.

BURT PRELUTSKY/Fiesta Salad

In My Mother's House, You Could Eat Off the Kitchen Floor (and If You Were Smart, You Ate the Kitchen Floor)

My mother had a green thumb. The unfortunate thing is that she employed it in the kitchen, and not the garden.

There are people, I'm aware, who are terror stricken at the mere thought of visiting a dentist. I, however, who am as prone to fear and panic as anyone and more than most, can snap my fingers at the drillmaster. It's all a matter of conditioning, you see. For, compared to some of the culinary disasters concocted by my mother, a drill isn't all that threatening. In fact, many was the time I used to wish I had anything, including cotton wadding, to nosh on, so long as my mother hadn't labored long and hard in its preparation.

We had a weekly dinner schedule in our house. Monday, we supped on hamburgers or lamb chops; we could tell them apart because the chops had one big bone, and the hamburger had hundreds of tiny ones. On Tuesday, we had salmon patties. On Wednesday, we'd receive a CARE package from the local deli. Thursday, we had tuna fish and leftovers. Friday was our night for boiled chicken and barley soup. I don't recall what, besides indigestion, we had on the weekend.

If my mother could be said to have had specialties, they would have been her Tuesday and Friday night offerings. I don't know who first invented the salmon patty, but he must have been blood kin to the nudnick who created chipped beef on toast. My mother used to sweat over those darn salmon patties. Which didn't help their flavor any, but probably didn't hurt, either. At dinner she glowered at me as I stared at the orange-and-yellow creations, trying to determine, in 20 Questions fashion, whether the things would qualify as animal, vegetable or mineral.

My mother would remind me on such occasions that children were starving in Europe. I would urge her to mail my dinner to Poland. The nice part about the plan was that the patties wouldn't have required wrapping. Put a stamp on one of those little beauties and it could have been mailed intact to starving children on the moon.

As if Tuesday night weren't hardship enough, Wednesday my lunch bag would contain a salmon patty on stale white bread. On Wednesday, believe me, I was quite prepared to keep the salmon patties and mail my mother to Europe.

It was on Friday, though, that she truly outdid herself. There are people, I understand, who absolutely adore barley soup. Which only proves, as the missionary said to the cannibal chief, that there's no accounting for taste.

I was able to hold a spoonful of barley soup in my mouth for a remarkably long period. I could probably have kept it in there for a month, if one can possibly survive a month without swallowing. Actually, I would eventually swallow the soup; that is, the liquid portion. I would manage this by slowly and ever so carefully filtering the liquid through my teeth. This would leave me, though, with a mouthload of barley. Which I would no sooner swallow than hemlock. After about half an hour, my parents would finally cave in. The soup would be removed from my presence and the entree would be served. It is hard to describe boiled chicken to those whom fate has spared. But such a chicken, you can safely assume, doesn't go to barnyard heaven. The only creature sorrier than a boiled chicken is the poor soul who's expected to attack it with gusto and delight.

It always seemed to me that this country missed a golden opportunity to end World War II long before 1945 rolled around. It would have meant sneaking my mother into the kitchen of the German High Command. As I see this daring plan taking shape, by Tuesday night, there would have been a vague, but general, queasiness among the members of the group. By Wednesday, when Goebbels and Goering discovered salmon patty sandwiches in their lunch bags, morale would have been plummeting. And, by Friday evening, when even Der Fuhrer himself would have been sitting with a mouthful of barley, while my mother was noodging him about all the starving children in Milwaukee, you could have started the countdown to unconditional surrender.

Fiesta Salad

• Serves 6

Head of iceberg lettuce, washed, drained and broken into bite-size pieces
3 or 4 tomatoes, cut into wedges
1 avocado, peeled and sliced
6 fresh green onions, chopped
Garlic salt to taste (or a fresh clove or 2 of garlic, put through garlic press)
Salt to taste
1 tablespoon jalapeno pepper juice
Bag of corn chips (7 ounce size and use quantity desired—Original Fritos are best)
Cheese sauce (recipe at right).

Cheese Sauce for Dressing:

In top of double boiler over simmering water, melt:

¼ pound cheddar cheese
⅓ cup evaporated milk (more if thinner sauce is desired)

Method: When ready to serve, toss together lettuce, tomatoes, avocado, green onions, garlic salt (or fresh garlic), and salt, jalapeno pepper juice and corn chips. Pour melted cheese sauce over salad.

25

JOAN RIVERS/Pears and Caviar

A Triumph Over Circumstances

After Melissa was born, I wanted to know everything I could about feeding a child. The doctor told me that the age that a baby learns to sit up, stand up, and walk, varies greatly. "Temperament and weight," he said, "have a great deal to do with it. For instance, a fat baby may not have much of a yen to get moving very fast."

Didn't I know it! I was such a fat baby, I had barely reached the sitting up stage when it was time for me to go to camp. My parents had to take me there in a U-Haul. As a kid, I ate so many sweets and lost so many teeth at once that the tooth fairy at our house had a hernia.

I was determined that Melissa would grow up with first-rate eating habits, but no matter what I did, I couldn't figure out what was wrong with her. Once I prepared a great meal for her: lamp chops, spinach, mashed potatoes, ice cream, and she wouldn't touch it. Boy, was I upset! If that kid only knew how many hours it took me to stuff that into the bottle.

In spite of everything, I am proud to say that Melissa has grown up with a wonderful healthy appetite. To get across the notion that eating can be enjoyable, in my house we just say, "Eat some more, kid. It's good. Mommy didn't make it." The way I figure it, if women were meant to slave over a hot stove, they would have been given aluminum hands.

Pears and Caviar

Pear halves, cored (allow ½ pear per person)
Sugar
Beluga Caviar (large grain, grey)
Lettuce leaves
Lemon wedges

Method: Poach pear halves till barely tender in small amount of water. Cool and drain. Sprinkle each pear half with sugar. Fill cavity of each with a mound of caviar. Arrange each pear half on a bed of lettuce. Decorate with a wedge of lemon.

Serve as hors d'oeuvre or as first course for a luncheon.

When fresh pears are not in season, substitute canned pears and omit sugar.

NEIL SIMON/Cole Slaw

My Mother's Big Hit

It's a known fact that mothers have an anxiety to please.

When I was young, my mother once asked me if I liked chocolate pudding, and I said yes. For the next 15 days she served me chocolate pudding for dessert. Finally I said that I didn't want any more pudding. And my mother said, "But I thought you liked it."

My Mother the Angel (a Conversation with Mrs. Simon)

When Neil decided he no longer wanted to do TV shows, he wrote his first Broadway play, *Come Blow Your Horn*. He said, "Ma, I'm going to make you an angel." And he put $500 in the play in my name. Needless to say, the play was a success. He re-invested the money in his next play—and next and next and next, and so on. As far as angels go, I guess I'm a little better off than most.

Cole Slaw • Serves 6

1 medium green head cabbage, including outer leaves, sliced thinly or shredded
1 carrot, grated
About ½ cup mayonnaise
1 or 2 tablespoons vinegar (to taste)
Sugar
Salt

Toss ingredients together.

For a delicious variation of this basic recipe, try adding:

½ cup drained pineapple chunks, fresh or canned
½ cup walnut meats
1 ripe Kiwi

Method: Arrange cold slaw in an attractive bowl. Peel and slice a ripe kiwi. Arrange slices on top of the cole slaw. Decorate with sprigs of mint.

PETER YARROW/"You Are What You Eat" Salad Dressing

The Ballad of the Salad

In 1966, I found myself on a local TV cooking show in Texas while promoting my film *You Are What You Eat*. "Can you cook?" I was asked.

The answer was affirmative, but I had to figure out a way to get in a plug for my movie while doing it. An oven light went on over my head. Why not sing a song from the picture? So, wearing an apron, and working without Paul and Mary, I started to sing a cappella. It was like the Barber of Seville singing while giving a haircut, only I was doing my thing while mixing a sauce for the salad.

The more vigorous my mixing got, the faster the tempo of my singing became. When I pampered the salad, I pampered the song.

It may not have been the most stirring recital I've ever done, but I did get to plug the picture—and the TV crew loved the dressing.

Funny, though—no one praised my singing!

"You Are What You Eat" Salad Dressing
• Serves 6-8

1 cup sour cream
½ cup mayonnaise
Juice of 1 lemon
Fresh dill or tarragon, minced fine
Salt
Fresh ground pepper

Method: Combine sour cream, mayonnaise, lemon juice and dill or tarragon. Season with salt and freshly ground pepper. Serve over lettuce and tomato salad.

MEAT

LUCILLE BALL • Goulash
BINNIE BARNES • Potboiler
ART BUCHWALD • Brisket of Beef
GEORGE BURNS • Baked Lima Beans with
Flanken
NEIL DIAMOND • Gedempte Fleish (Beef Pot
Roast)
TOTIE FIELDS • Mish Mosh
SID GILLMAN • Team Spaghetti Sauce
HANK GREENBERG • Beef Stew Mamilige
BUDDY HACKETT • Cholent (Stew)
MONTY HALL • Sweet and Sour Stewed Tongue
STUBBY KAYE • Stuffed Veal Pocket

ABBE LANE • Sweet and Sour Meat Dish
MERVYN LeROY • Kekletten (Beef Patties)
ROBERT Q. LEWIS • Stuffed Cabbage
SHARI LEWIS • Roast Leg of Lamb
ROBERT MERRILL • Beef Brisket
JAN MURRAY • Steak Tartare
JEAN NIDETCH • Meatball Ragout
LOUIS NYE • Sauerkraut Stew
AVERY SCHREIBER • Tongue
SANDOR STERN • Beef Soy Stew
SUSAN STRASBERG • Sweet and Sour Stuffed
Peppers
LEON URIS • Braised Lamb Shanks
BOBBY VAN • Kreplach
BARBARA WALTERS • Stuffed Cabbage
HENNY YOUNGMAN • Sweet and Sour Ragout

LUCILLE BALL/Goulash

Thirty Seconds over Swan Lake by Gary Morton

I always had a recurring dream about Swan Lake in the Catskill Mountains. Swan Lake, in case you didn't know, is surrounded by a cluster of kosher hotels. I dreamed that the lake was filled with borscht and that I was in an airplane bombing it with boiled potatoes.

My mother made the worst vegetables, and I subsequently have hated vegetables all my life. She would let the peas and carrots boil for three hours. I was an adult before I knew there was such a thing as a hard carrot.

Lucy loves cheese blintzes, which I introduced to her. I am in constant search for a blintz connection. All of our friends who cook them send them over for us. One day we had about 35 blintzes in the freezer. Lucy reheats them and then sits down with a lot of sour cream and enjoys! Her favorite dishes are blintzes and, being a loyal New Englander, pot roast. Culinarily, she has the best of two worlds.

Goulash • Serves 4-6

2 bunches green onions, chopped
2 large green peppers, chopped
½ clove garlic, choped (or put through garlic press)
2 or 3 tablespoons margarine
2 pounds lean ground round steak or other lean beef
1 large (#2½ = 3½ cups) can, solid pack tomatoes
Salt and pepper to taste
¼ teaspoon monosodium glutamate
½ pound small egg noodles, cooked and drained

Method: Saute chopped green onions, green peppers and garlic in margarine. Add ground beef. Combine with vegetables and brown meat. Add can of solid pack (juice, too) tomatoes. Season with salt, pepper or monosodium glutamate. Bring mixture to boil; then reduce heat to simmer. Allow to cook till all flavors are well combined—about 1 hour. Last half-hour of cooking, add the cooked egg noodles.

BINNIE BARNES/Potboiler

Potpourri

I was the youngest of 16 children. My father, who was Jewish, was a London bobby; and my mother, though born in London, was a Florentine who knew from birth what to do with pasta.

I was brought up half and half. It was not unlikely that we confused the prayers before eating —a motzi before the pasta and a Hail Mary before a knish.

Potboiler   • Serves 12-14

2 large knockwurst, cut into 12 or 14 chunks
3 or 4 pounds corned beef
2 stewing chickens, excess fat removed, cut into 12 or 14 serving pieces
  Sufficient water to cover meat and chicken parts
1 large cabbage, cut into chunks
  Sufficient water to cover cabbage
5-6 cups cooked rice (start with 2 cups uncooked rice and cook per directions on package)
12-14 whole medium onions, peeled
12-14 medium potatoes, peeled
12-14 carrots, peeled
Sufficient water to cover onions, potatoes and carrots
2 or 3 hard-cooked eggs, sliced or quartered
Salt to taste

Method: Cover knockwurst, corned beef and stewing chickens with water and cook till meat and chickens are tender. Drain meats. Slice corned beef. Reserve liquid from meat. Remove excess fat (this may be done easily if liquid is chilled in refrigerator till fat sets). Cook cabbage in water to cover until tender. Drain cabbage. Reserve liquid. Cook 2 cups rice according to package instructions. Cook onions, potatoes and carrots in sufficient water to cover. Cook till vegetables are tender. Drain, reserving liquid. In a large soup kettle or roasting pan (boiler), pour all the reserved liquids (taste to see if salt is required). Add cabbage and rice. Top with cooked onions, carrots and potatoes. Layer the sliced corned beef, chicken parts and knockwurst over the vegetables. Heat. Decorate top with sliced or quartered hard-cooked eggs. Serve in large soup bowls.

ART BUCHWALD/Brisket of Beef

Chicken about Beef

My Aunt Molly used to make brisket of beef and every time we went to her house for dinner, we could not eat all that day because Aunt Molly got enraged if we did not take three portions apiece. Her eyes would dart from one person to another, and God help us if our plates were empty. Since then I have had very mixed feelings about brisket of beef. I like it, but it frightens me.

Brisket of Beef • Serves 10 hungry people

6-7 pound fresh brisket of beef, excess fat trimmed

Use pan with rack. In bottom of pan, put the following chopped vegetables:

1 large onion
1 green pepper
1 parsnip
3 celery stalks
2 carrots
 Seasoning (Season-All salt) to taste
3-4 cups boiling water

2 tablespoons catsup
½ cup sherry or other wine
 Parsley and radish roses for garnish

Method: Season trimmed brisket with Season-All salt. Add 3 cups boiling water and catsup to vegetables in bottom of pan. Place rack over vegetables and put brisket, fat side up, on rack. Cover pan with aluminum foil and puncture holes in foil with a fork. Place in 450-degree oven for 30 minutes. Reduce heat to 350 degrees and roast 3 to 3½ hours or until meat is fork tender. Add more water during roasting if necessary. Add sherry or other wine when meat is almost done (last half-hour of cooking). Puree vegetables and liquid in pan for gravy. Keep hot while you slice meat thin with an electric knife. Arrange meat on warm serving platter. Garnish with parsley and radish roses. Pass gravy.

What, no garlic! If you would like to add garlic, squeeze a clove or two in your garlic press and season meat with garlic and Season-All at the same time. Or add to liquid with vegetables. Flavor will mellow in cooking.

GEORGE BURNS/Baked Lima Beans with Flanken

Depression Banquet

When I was seven years old, I was in the Pee Wee Quartet. We sang in bars and on the Staten Island ferry, and when we were real good we entered contests. If we won, the first prize was usually $5—$1.25 a piece. I came from a family of 12, and on $1.25 we could eat for a week. We'd go to the bakery and get huge Vienna rolls, real big. They were two for a penney, so for 6¢ the whole family feasted. Those Vienna rolls were so big we're still eating them.

Baked Lima Beans with Flanken

• Serves 6-8 as a side dish

(**To make milchig, leave out flanken. Add butter or oil and season with curry. You may want less sugar if curry is used.**)

1 pound lima beans
1 pound flanken (Have butcher cut meat away from bones in thin strips. Leave the fat on; it will add flavor)
1 teaspoon salt, or to taste
  Pepper to taste
1 small onion, chopped
1 tablespoon oil or fat
1 cup liquid from the cooked beans
1½ cups tomato juice
1 clove garlic
  About ½ cup brown sugar, or to taste

Method: Cook lima beans as directed on package, adding flanken bone, salt and pepper. Cook until limas are almost tender and flavor has been extracted from flanken bone. Remove bone. Saute meat strips and small onion in 1 tablespoon oil or fat. Drain limas, retaining 1 cup of liquid. Combine limas, cup of liquid, tomato juice, clove of garlic, sugar and the sauteed meat strips and onion. Correct seasoning with salt, pepper and sugar to taste. Bake about 2 hours in 325-degree oven in an earthenware casserole that has a close-fitting lid.
  Nice for a buffet.

NEIL DIAMOND/Gedempte Fleish (Beef Pot Roast)

Wall-to-Wall Papering

In my grandmother's home and the homes of many Jewish families, it was customary to clean the house and wash the floors on Friday. No sooner did the floors dry than they were covered with newspapers so they would stay clean. As any New York Jewish family can tell you—for they are all connoisseurs of linoleum "paper placement"—it is much better to spread out the *New York Times* than the *Daily News*. Not only does the *Times* cover more area, but since it has fewer pictures and black on the pages, it leaves fewer smudges when you remove it.

On Fridays, at Grandmother's, I used to play "reading hopscotch." I'd get down on all fours and crawl around like an infant to catch up on current events.

We never saw the linoleum until the next week when it was time to wash the floors again. In our minds, clean newspapers on the floor meant a yuntifdik (holiday) feeling.

And, for the life of me, I don't remember what color our floors were.

Gedempte Fleish (Beef Pot Roast) • Serves 5

1 package onion soup mix
1 cup water
2 slices chuck, approximately 2 pounds each
1 teaspoon salt, or to taste
½ teaspoon black pepper, or to taste
1 teaspoon minced garlic or to taste
6 potatoes, cut in quarters
1 green pepper, cut in quarters
6 carrots, cut in quarters
2 stalks celery, cut in quarters
Dash of catsup

Method: In a large skillet, dissolve onion soup mix in cup of water. Trim off fat and cut meat into bite-size pieces. Add to onion soup mix. Season with salt, pepper and garlic. Cover and simmer 1 hour. Lay potatoes, pepper, carrots, celery across top of simmering meat. Sprinkle catsup on top of meat and vegetables and cook another 1½ hours.

Side dishes: Serve potato pancakes, or kasha varnishkas, or crumble matzo into bowl and cover with gravy from pot roast.

TOTIE FIELDS/Mish Mosh

Doggone-It

My sister Rosie is the cook in the family. In Las Vegas where I live, just before one Thanksgiving she cooked up a regular storm. Mushroom and barley soup, brisket, noodle pooding—all the typical Thanksgiving dishes. (You never saw a Jewish pilgrim?) That Thanksgiving, since our refrigerator and freezer were full of food, we put the holiday food into big boxes and stored it overnight in the garage, which in Vegas in November is colder than my refrigerator. The next day we went to the garage to bring the food into the house. To our horror, we saw the food strewn all over the garage. The gardener had left the garage door open and a dog, attracted by the aroma of Rosie's delicacies, had devoured everything. In his best years, Rin-Tin-Tin never ate so well.

We went out to dinner and afterward drove around the neighborhood looking for the dog so that we could give the owner a piece of our mind. How would we know the dog? Easy. All we had to do was find a dog with heartburn!

Mish Mosh • Serves 6

3 onions, chopped
3 tablespoons oil
2 pounds hamburger
  Pepper and garlic to taste
1 box egg noodles (8-10 ounces.)
4 eggs, beaten
1 cup onion soup (made from ½ package onion soup mix, combine with sufficient water to make one cup)
  Salt to taste

Method: Saute onions in oil. Add hamburger to onion mixture, season with pepper and garlic. Stir fry until brown. Cook egg noodles according to package instructions; drain, and mix with beaten eggs. Combine meat and noodle mixture; add onion soup and water mixture. Bake in large greased casserole 1 hour at 350 degrees.

Don't forget that the onion soup mix is salty. Season after you have added the onion soup mix to the other ingredients.

SID GILLMAN/Team Spaghetti Sauce

The Search

Talk about food and my youth in Minneapolis and three things come to mind: quarts of milk, lots of eggs and the search. Let me explain.

I was a terrible eater. None of the wonderful old country dishes my mother made appealed to me, but milk, I would drink milk. Do you remember the old-fashioned bottles with two sections, the cream on top and the milk underneath? I would knock two of them off in the morning. Holding a bottle by the neck in one hand, I inverted it with my head tilted back and a steady stream went down my throat. Eggs I could eat by the dozen. The only way I varied this diet was to have them sunny-side up one day and scrambled the next. Now let me explain the search.

While I didn't like the traditional dishes, I loved my mother's pastries. She could make strudel mandelbroit and kichel like nobody's business. As soon as she made it I would make it disappear, so she decided to hide it and then the game began, with my mother hiding the strudel and me searching for it. Many times she faked me out of position by telling me she hadn't baked that day. But, on Friday, I knew she baked something special for Friday night and I tore the house apart from attic to basement looking for strudel under the rafters and in the closets.

Even though I was a food-devouring machine I never had an extra ounce of fat on me during my football playing and coaching days. It's only been these last years at San Diego and Houston where I couldn't keep up with the kids on the field that I started to become a nervous eater and put on a little weight.

One footnote on why I hate borscht. My mother used to make wine, pickles and borscht all in large, individual vats. One day while hunting for strudel I fell into the vat of borscht. It didn't taste good then and I haven't tasted it since.

Team Spaghetti Sauce
• Serves 12

2-4 tablespoons olive oil (to cover bottom of
   kettle, optional)
3 pounds leanest ground beef
3 large onions, chopped
1 pound fresh mushrooms, sliced
2 cloves garlic, crushed
3 12-ounce cans tomato paste
2 #2½ cans Italian-style tomatoes
   Scant teaspoon cinnamon
1 teaspoon crushed red Italian peppers (or less—
   these are hot)
   Salt, to taste
1 teaspoon sugar
2-3 tablespoons or less, to taste
   Sweet basil, to taste
   Rosemary, to taste

Method: If desired, cover bottom of large kettle with olive oil. Add ground meat, crumbled, and brown until its color turns. Add chopped onion and mushrooms, saute. Add garlic, tomato paste, tomatoes and seasonings. Blend. Simmer for 2-3 hours, adjusting seasoning to taste.

After cooking, sauce improves if allowed to sit for several hours.

HANK GREENBERG/Beef Stew Mamilige

No Business for a Nice Jewish Boy

My mother was a typical orthodox Roumanian Jewish lady. She baked her own bread, made chicken and chicken soup for Friday and blessed the candles. Passover dinner was a traumatic experience —waiting for my father to finish the four questions and the prayers while we all starved to death. We dipped our fingers in the wine and tasted, and by the time my father was finished, some of us were tipsy. And someone always got spanked.

When I was playing ball in high school, spending my weekends on the field (defaming the Sabbath), coming home dirty and bedraggled, the neighbors weren't so tolerant. Their gossiping was always the same. "The Greenbergs are such a nice family. It's a shame one of them had to be such a bum."

Beef Stew Mamilige • Serves 6

3 pounds stewing beef, cut in large pieces
1 teaspoon salt
  Pepper to taste
3 medium onions, chopped
2 leeks, cut up (white part only)
2 tablespoons oil or other fat
3 cloves garlic, put through garlic press
1 bay leaf
½ teaspoon thyme
2 ounces brandy
2 cans beef broth
1 cup Burgundy wine
2 carrots, sliced
2 tablespoons chopped parsley

Method: Season meat with salt and pepper. In a Dutch oven or heavy pan, saute chopped onions and leeks in 2 tablespoons oil till onions are golden brown. Add seasoned meat, crushed garlic, bay leaf and ½ teaspoon thyme. Toss to combine, and brown meat. Add brandy and set aflame. Spoon till flame subsides. Add beef broth, Burgundy wine and carrots. Bring to boil. Reduce heat to simmer meat and allow to cook until meat is tender (about 2 hours). Correct seasoning with salt and pepper. Remove bay leaf. Sprinkle with chopped parsley and serve.

Mamilige

• Serves 6

4 cups water
1 teaspoon salt
2 cups cornmeal
4 tablespoons margarine

Method: Bring water to boil. Add salt. Add corn-meal slowly, stirring constantly. Reduce heat. Cook, stirring till mixture thickens. Add margarine. Continue to cook till mixture leaves sides of pan. Stir occasionally during cooking. Turn out on a platter. Serve with gravy from stew.

BUDDY HACKETT/Cholent (Stew)

Eating Cholent

Cholent is not a Southern California dish. The only time Southern Californians eat this dish is when they're going skiing for the weekend and they'll be subject to extreme cold and have no tolerance for it.

Also, eating cholent is good for anyone who doesn't own an overcoat and is going to the East.

You take the cholent along in a jar. You eat it on the plane when they serve dinner. When you land in New York in any cold degrees they got, you're warm inside, and that'll last you long enough to go out and buy an overcoat. You don't even need a snow shovel. When you walk in the snow for the first three hours after eating cholent, snow will melt and water will run wherever you step.

You're not to be frightened by what takes place in your chest after eating cholent. You're not to call the fire department or think that the hot Santa Ana winds are upon you. Because that's a natural phenomenon—eating cholent three days in a row (it's only supposed to be eaten on Shabbas for the afternoon meal) makes you a lightning machine. In fact, the true story about Benjamin Franklin has nothing to do with a key or a kite. Actually, he ate a cholent a neighbor gave him and became a lightning conductor.

Cholent (Stew)

Requires at least 5 hours preparation.

3 pounds flanken or brisket
3 tablespoons rendered fat from the meat or other fat or oil
3 onions, cut up
2-3 cloves garlic, crushed in garlic press
2 cups dried lima beans and
1 cup chick peas, combined and covered with cold water and soaked overnight
2-3 celery stalks, cut up
3-4 carrots in chunks
3-4 potatoes, in chunks (optional)
    About 2 tablespoons salt, to taste
¼ teaspoon pepper, to taste
¼ teaspoon ginger (optional)
    Cinnamon—sprinkle to taste

Method: Put 3 tablespoons fat in a large, heavy saucepan with a good-fitting lid (Dutch oven is perfect). Get it hot. Add onions, brown them well. Add meat, brown. Season with salt, pepper and crushed garlic. Drain lima beans and chick peas. Set liquid aside. Add lima beans, chick peas, celery, carrots and potatoes (if used). Add ginger and cinnamon, if desired. Toss to combine. Then add liquid drained from beans and peas (mixture should be covered to 1 inch above the solids in the pot). Bring liquid to boil. Cover pan and put in slow 225- to 250-degree oven for 24 hours. *Or*, if you are in a hurry, you may cook in 350-degree oven for 5 or 6 hours.

MONTY HALL/Sweet and Sour Stewed Tongue

Hall's Mark of Distinction

My grandmother never measured. She'd take a "handful of this," and a "pinch of that" and throw it in! *Her* cupful was never *anybody else's* cupful. There seems to be a code among venerable Jewish ladies: they have an intuitive sense of exact measurement and quantity. They know by texture exactly when the dough is right. I remember there was always a lot of pounding and rolling and flour flying around the kitchen. My grandmother once gave a recipe to a non-Jewish neighbor, and in her typical nonspecific way said, "A bisel mehr, a bisel wenegar" (English translation: "More or less"). The neighbor baked the cake and was appalled at the result. It was so bitter it was inedible. The neighbor couldn't find the mehr, but she sure used the vinegar!

My mother, on the other hand, combined her great insight into human nature with her cooking talent. When we were first married, my bride Marilyn faced a tremendous challenge in equaling my mother's reputation as an outstanding Jewish cook. I urged Marilyn to get my mother's recipes, and so we invited her over to cook her specialty. The dish was a fiasco. I was nonplussed. How had it tasted so good when I was a boy? What had happened? But my mother's brilliant mind had conceived a plan to make my wife's cooking look good by comparison. She had deliberately cooked everything just a little off. She threw the game!

Sweet and Sour Stewed Tongue • Serves 4

1 fresh beef tongue
   Water to cover
1 tablespoon salt
1 onion, sliced
6 whole cloves
6 peppercorns
2 bay leaves
1 onion, chopped fine
1 tablespoon fat
1 tablespoon flour
2 cups tongue liquid
1 tablespoon finely ground almonds
1 stick cinnamon

3 cloves
2 tablespoons raisins
¼ cup brown sugar
1 tablespoon molasses
  Juice of 1 lemon

Method: Place tongue in pot with hot or cold water to cover. Add salt, sliced onion, cloves, peppercorns, bay leaves. Cover pot and let simmer 3 to 4 hours until tender. (Add hot water if necessary to keep tongue covered during cooking.) Remove from heat; let tongue stand in liquid until cool enough to handle. Peel off outer skin, trim off root and return tongue to liquid. When ready to serve, set aside 2 cups tongue liquid and slice the tongue. Saute chopped onion in 1 tablespoon fat until onion is golden. Sprinkle flour over onion. Cook, stirring for a few minutes. Gradually add 2 cups tongue liquid, stirring constantly. Cook and stir 5 minutes till mixture is well blended and slightly thickened. Add almonds, cinnamon, cloves and raisins. Combine well. Add brown sugar, molasses and lemon juice. Cook and stir 10 minutes longer. Correct seasoning, adding more salt, sugar and lemon juice if desired. Add sliced tongue. Heat thoroughly and serve immediately in the sauce.

STUBBY KAYE/Stuffed Veal Pocket

The Jersey Bounce

We always had to shlep 35 or 40 miles over to New Jersey from the Bronx to a relative's house for Passover. My Uncle Simon performed the seder in the old-fashioned style. He did the full nine innings. No pinch hitters allowed. There was no shortening of the service due to rain or hunger. I used to sit there and die from hunger until he got through with the eggs and parsley.

I went for two reasons—the meal and the prizes that were hidden around. Because I was the fattest kid in the family, the others almost always beat me to the prizes. There was always a lot of noise because there were approximately 18 people at the seder and just as many dogs.

Somewhere after the prizes and between the arrival of Elijah through the open door, I used to fall asleep on the couch and had to be shlepped all the way back to the Bronx. Once I woke up in the middle of an argument between my mother and father. Each was saying, "You carry him this year! I carried him last year!"

Stuffed Veal Pocket • Serves 6-8

4-6 pound veal roast (have the butcher make a "pocket")
1½ teaspoons salt
¼ teaspoon pepper (or to taste)
1 teaspoon paprika
  Potato stuffing (recipe follows)
1 clove garlic, put through garlic press or minced fine
1 tablespoon melted fat, oil or margarine
1 tablespoon Kitchen Bouquet

1 onion, cut into slices
1 cup boiling water
  Crab apples for garnish

Stuffing for Veal Pocket

Combine:

1½ cups grated potatoes, drained
1 egg
1 onion, grated
1 teaspoon salt
  Pepper to taste

Method: Season veal roast with salt, pepper and paprika. Stuff pocket in roast with the potato stuffing. Skewer closed or sew. Spread minced or crushed garlic over roast. Combine tablespoon of melted fat with Kitchen Bouquet and baste roast with mixture. Put sliced onion and 1 cup boiling water in a roasting pan. Add seasoned, stuffed veal roast and roast meat in 325-degree oven, covered, for 1 hour. Then remove cover, continue to roast till meat is tender. This will take another 1½ to 2½ hours, depending on size of roast. Baste often after cover is removed. Serve with spiced crab apples.

ABBE LANE/Sweet and Sour Meat Dish

The Timid Eater

I remember going to my paternal grandmother's house for the weekends. My grandmother was German and lived her life in typical German thrift. She was very sweet and always tried to please, so the stereotyped German authoritarian attitude of "You *will* eat!" was alien to her. Her method was much more subtle and much more effective.

If you didn't eat what was put in front of you for dinner, you would get it next morning for breakfast. And if you didn't eat it at breakfast, you would get it for lunch.

It had such a profound effect on me that to this day, even when I order a favorite dish that I know I could devour endlessly, I order only small portions. I'm always afraid that if I don't clean up my plate, I will have to eat the leftovers at the next meal.

Sweet and Sour Meat Dish • Serves 4

2 pounds chuck
2 large marrow bones
2 1-pound cans of whole beets, drained
1 whole medium onion
1½ cups water
4 medium potatoes
2 or 3 pieces of sour salt, to taste (It may be advisable to start with 2 and add the third piece if necessary.)
2 or 3 cloves garlic, crushed
3 tablespoons sugar, (to taste)
Salt, to taste
Pepper, to taste

Method: Season chuck meat and marrow bones with salt and pepper. Add drained beets. Add 1½ cups water. Bring to boil. Reduce heat, cover and simmer till meat is barely tender. Add garlic, sour salt, potatoes and onions. Bring to boil. Reduce heat and continue to cook till meat and potatoes are tender. Season with sugar. Add salt and pepper to taste.

MERVYN LeROY/Kekletten (Beef Patties)

My First Roast

I was born on the kitchen table in the house—62 Geary Street in San Francisco—that was my home until the '06 quake wrecked it. My mother was a slight woman, and when I arrived on the scene, I weighed only two and a half pounds. The doctor who attended my mother took one look at me and said that if I was to survive they would have to take desperate measures. "The best thing is to put him in a turkey roasting pan, put it in the oven, and keep him there. Make sure the flame is real low, however."

Maybe I was the world's first stove-incubator baby. My adoring parents, grandparents, aunts and uncles stood around the stove, peeking in the oven door to see if I was done—or alive.

As I think back to my childhood, I recall that my mother's favorite dish was something she called "kekletten," pronounced "kekletten." I say it was her favorite not to indicate that she liked the taste of it better than anything else, but she made it more than anything else. Now that I think back, I don't think she ever made anything else.

Now, as I continue to reflect on my youth, for the first time I am aware that "kekletten" is a plural form of the word "keklet," and since Momma never served one of anything, and therefore we never ate less than one of anything, I shall assume that kekletten is always plural.

Momma's kekletten very simply were chopped meat patties, fried in chicken fat, but a more descriptive definition would be "hand grenades."

Kekletten (Beef Patties)   • Makes 4 patties

1 pound ground beef
1 onion, chopped and sauteed in 1 tablespoon chicken fat
1 slice stale white bread soaked in ¼ cup water
1 egg
1 clove garlic, crushed
Salt and pepper to taste
2-3 tablespoons chicken fat
½ cup breadcrumbs

Method: Combine all ingredients except chicken fat and bread crumbs. Make patties of the meat mixture. Roll in bread crumbs. Fry in chicken fat.

ROBERT Q. LEWIS/Stuffed Cabbage

My Favorite Intermission

When I got my own apartment, I went up to Mother's for dinner one night. She had made stuffed cabbage. "Listen," I said, "make me a batch of stuffed cabbage so I can put it in the freezer, and whenever I want it I can just heat it up." About a week later, I got out the stuffed cabbage—as I recall, it was about a dozen servings—and I ate it all. Afterwards, I went into the hospital.

Here are Mrs. Lewis' cabbage rolls—to be eaten in judicious quantities.

Stuffed Cabbage
• Serves 6

1½ pounds ground beef
½ cup cooked rice
1 onion, grated
¼ cup water (optional. Will make meat mixture softer)
Salt and pepper to taste

1 large cabbage, separated into leaves and put into boiling water for a few minutes to wilt. Remove from water and cool enough to handle comfortably.
Tomato sauce (recipe below)

Sauce
Combine in a roasting pan with a lid:

6 small (6 ounce) cans tomato sauce
1 can water
1⅓ cups brown sugar
1 cup cider vinegar
14 gingersnaps, softened in hot water

Method: Combine meat, rice, grated onion, water (if used) and salt and pepper. Put a mound of meat mixture into each cabbage leaf. Wrap, completely enclosing meat. Place each rolled cabbage leaf, seam down, into the tomato sauce. Cover and cook slowly 3 hours. (It may be necessary to thin sauce with hot water.)

SHARI LEWIS/Roast Leg of Lamb

Short Story

I found my grandmother's kosher cooking very boring. Every Friday night she would boil a chicken to death. I enjoyed playing with that chicken's flexible feet much more than I did eating its tender but tasteless body. (What has happened to chicken feet? Why don't they get boiled in the soup any more? Are they now breeding footless fowl that just shimmy along wire netting on their chests?)

Now my grandmother was no cook, but she *was* some strong-willed short lady! She had produced fourteen children, eight had survived, and they and their offspring were *expected* at her table for Shabbat dinner.

My teen-aged girl cousins and I finally decided that Friday night would be the night we dieted in preparation for the indulgences of the weekend. Since we each weighed 89 pounds or less, my Mama took over the cooking for us "little ones" (we all were short).

The following is what she concocted for the spicy palates of those second-generation Americans—succulent, savory, with a seductive aroma that will entice you to the table!

Roast Leg of Lamb   • Serves 8

6-pound leg of lamb, seasoned with salt and
    pepper
½ cup Dijon-type mustard
1 tablespoon soy sauce
1 clove mashed garlic
1 teaspoon ground thyme
¼ teaspoon powdered ginger
2 tablespoons olive oil

Method: Blend all ingredients except oil. Beat in oil (in droplets) to make mayonnaise-like cream. Hours before roasting, brush this cream on leg of lamb. Set on roasting pan rack. Roast at 350 degrees for 1 to 1¼ hours to desired pinkness.

If lamb is preferred well done, reduce heat to 325 degrees and cook 25 to 30 minutes per pound.

ROBERT MERRILL/Beef Brisket

Aida Spaghetti

When ! was touring with the Met in *Aida*, in Cleveland we had a marvelous chef backstage who also happened to be the makeup man. He was called Poppa Senz, and he made wonderful spaghetti with garlic tomato sauce on a little stove in a small kitchen backstage.

In *Aida* I don't come on until late in the second act, about 9:30. So Poppa Senz said I shouldn't have dinner . . . I should come to the theatre and he'd make me spaghetti. I couldn't resist. I came to the theatre about 7:00, and he made unbelievable spaghetti, but I didn't realize he had put in an extra amount of garlic. I made my entrance onto the stage with the famous prima donna who played Aida, but when I walked over to embrace her, she took one whiff and slapped my face—I smelled so terrible from the garlic it gave her the vapors. When I looked into the wings, I saw Poppa Senz and the cast laughing. They knew she was allergic to garlic. The moral of the story is: Don't fool around with a prima donna.

Beef Brisket • Serves 4-6

3½ - to 4-pound brisket, trimmed of excess fat
Garlic powder (a sprinkle)
Onion powder (a sprinkle)
Meat tenderizer used according to package instructions
¼ teaspoon ground ginger
Juice of 1 lemon
3 tablespoons brown sugar
1 cup water
1 tablespoon flour (optional)

Method: Sprinkle brisket with garlic and onion powder and tenderizer. Put into roasting pan and cover with aluminum foil. Roast in 325-degree oven about 2½ to 3½ hours, depending on size of brisket. Turn frequently during roasting. When meat is almost tender, combine ground ginger, lemon juice, brown sugar and water. Pour over meat. Return to oven and cook uncovered 1 hour. Use sauce for gravy. If desired, gravy can be thickened with 1 tablespoon flour.

Slice meat for serving. Spoon some of juice over slices. Serve remaining juice in gravy boat.

JAN MURRAY/Steak Tartare

Ta Ta Tartare

When I was a young performer starting out in show business, I used to hear about the older performers eating at Sardi's, and they were always talking about tartare steak. It was the chic thing to eat.

I was living at home in the Bronx, so I asked my mother to make it for me. I didn't know what it was and she didn't know what it was. But I kept asking her until finally she said, "All right, all right, I'll make you tartare steak, and don't ever bother me again."

My mother was a typical Jewish mother, kept a kosher kitchen and, of course, cooked all meats well done. So I can imagine her distaste when she found out what it was and had to work with this raw meat.

I invited a friend of mine, a young agent named Harry Morton, over for dinner, announcing with great savoir faire that we were going to have tartare steak.

Out came the raw meat. We both turned green. Harry took a piece of bread in his mouth, held up his front "paws" and ran barking out of the house.

My mother's comment: "You eat that or I'll make you into tartare steak!"

Steak Tartare ● Serves 12

2 pounds raw, scraped or finely chopped fresh lean steak
2 raw egg yolks
½ cup finely chopped onions
4 mashed anchovies

Combine all the above and season to taste with:

Capers
Chopped parsley and other herbs
Olive oil
Worcestershire sauce

Method: Serve in mound garnished with parsley and/or anchovies. Or shape into small balls and roll in chopped parsley. Especially good with thinly sliced pumpernickel.

JEAN NIDETCH/Meatball Ragout

Wait and Watch Weight

I wasn't a pretty child, but I was a favorite with all my aunts because I loved and appreciated their cooking. The thought of lamb stew brought tears to my eyes.

I found my greatest excitement in eating since I was too fat to ride a bike or roller skate. By the time I was 38, I weighed 214 pounds. Then I decided that there must be a better way. I had spent most of my life overeating, and now I'm spending the rest of my life eating sensibly. Weight Watchers is watching me.

Meatball Ragout • Serves 1

8 ounces chopped beef or veal
1 teaspoon dehydrated onion flakes
¼ teaspoon Italian seasoning spice
1/8 teaspoon garlic powder

½ cup cooked or canned mushrooms, stems and pieces
1 cup zucchini, sliced
1 medium green pepper, cut in strips
¼ cup celery, thinly sliced
1 cup tomato juice
1 envelope instant beef broth and seasoning mix, or 1 beef bouillon cube
1 tablespoon dehydrated onion flakes
¼ teaspoon thyme
¼ teaspoon garlic powder

Method: Combine meat with onion flakes, Italian seasoning and garlic powder. Shape into balls, place on a rack and bake at 400 degrees approximately 10-15 minutes. Remove from oven and set aside. Combine the remaining ingredients in saucepan and simmer slowly. When mixture is reduced approximately one quarter in volume, add meatballs. Continue cooking until sauce is thick and meatballs are thoroughly heated.

LOUIS NYE/Sauerkraut Stew

Jenny Brings Home the Bacon

When I was a little boy, I was painfully thin, and my mother, Jenny, took me to all kinds of doctors to find some way of putting some meat on my bones. Finally, she heard of an Irish doctor who had had success fattening up emaciated children. Harboring no prejudice, my mother took me to the doctor. He had a ready solution—bacon. "Bacon?" my mother asked incredulously. The doctor nodded. In those days there was no such thing as kosher bacon.

We went home to inform my grandmother of the doctor's decision. When we entered our apartment she was in the corner with her scarf on her head and her prayer book in her hand. My mother hesitantly told her of the doctor's advice. My grandmother, who prayed day and night, was a hip and beautiful person and without flinching, she said, "If it's for our Label's health, buy it."

The three of us made a pact to keep this terrible fact from the rest of the family. My grandmother called it our "traifeneh secret." My mother bought separate plates and silverware so we shouldn't get it confused with our kosher wares. In those days the bacon was very thick and when she fried six slabs the smell of traif filled our house. The three of us, equipped with cardboard and newspapers, frenetically fanned the odor out the kitchen window. In all the neighborhood I was the healthiest-looking bar mitzvah boy.

Sauerkraut Stew • Serves 6

4-5 pounds flanken, excess fat trimmed off
1 large onion, chopped
2 tablespoons oil or schmaltz
1 pound sauerkraut and juice
1 sour green apple, diced
3 marrow bones (if possible)
1 cup water if necessary
Peeled potatoes, if desired
½ lemon
Sugar to taste (white or brown or even use honey)
Pepper to taste
Caraway seeds, if desired

Method: In big pot, brown flanken and onion in schmaltz or vegetable oil until onion is silvery. Add sauerkraut. Then add apple and marrow bones. Cover and cook until meat is almost tender (about 2 hours). Add extra water if needed, and potatoes if used. Squeeze juice of half a lemon into mixture and throw the lemon peel in too. Remove peel before serving. (The lemon peel gives a lovely, fresh flavor.) Add sugar or honey to taste and pepper and caraway seeds, if desired. No salt! Cover and cook till meat is tender and potatoes are cooked.

AVERY SCHREIBER/Tongue

Bite Your Tongue

What follows is the impossible-to-get recipe for Mama Min's Tongue . . . or, *My Mother's Tongue.* It's as gentle and heartwarming as a childhood memory.

I asked my mother to tell me where she got this recipe, and she said:

"When I first got married and wanted to invite my in-laws for my first dinner, I went to my Aunt Sarah and she gave it to me. She said that at a time when money was extremely scarce, it was very cheap, easy to make, and it went a good long way. I have been using it ever since. Although now it is not very cheap to make, it still goes a long way and seems to satisfy everyone."

I was lucky enough to marry a woman who loves tongue too, although she cooks it with a big "yuch!"

This recipe has never failed, and Jeff Wald, Helen Reddy's manager husband, has actually hired toughs to threaten me into saving him some every time my Mom visits. As of this writing, I am barricaded somewhere in Los Feliz, battling a regiment of his matron-like lackies (or is it lackettes?), who are storming the kitchen singing "I Am Woman."

My Mother's Tongue—An Ode

Georgie Jessel never knew, when he sang of "My
Mother's Eyes,"
How such a dish could sound so weird as a culinary
surprise.
Imagine opening up a pot, a teensy weensy crack
To take a look and then to find the food was
looking back.

Tongue
• Serves 6

**This dish should be prepared several days in
advance.**
1 beef tongue, 4-4½ pound (raw)

Method: Cook tongue in salted water until meat is
tender to the fork. Remove from pot, run under
cold water and remove white outer skin. (Broth in
which tongue is cooked can be used to make
excellent vegetable, barley and mushroom soup.)

Sauce

1 bunch carrots, sliced thin
1 stalk celery, diced not too small
2-3 onions, diced
1 large #2½ can whole tomatoes, cut up
**1 large can mushrooms (stems and pieces), or ½
pound fresh mushrooms**
Salt and pepper to taste
**Enough catsup to give a good, rich red color and
taste**

Method: Cook all sauce ingredients (adding enough
water to cover vegetables) until the vegetables are
done and you have a thick sauce. This takes
several hours over a very low flame. When tongue
is cold enough to slice nicely, put a layer of sauce
in a pot, follow with a layer of tongue, alternate
sauce and tongue ending with the sauce on top.
Prepare a few days before needed. The longer the
tongue steeps in the sauce, the tastier it is. Reheat
in 350-degree oven for ½ hour.

Other vegetables, such as peas, string beans or
whatever may also be added to the sauce to make a
more complete meal.

SANDOR STERN/Beef Soy Stew

Love at First Bite

Some years ago, I arrived in Toronto to begin a university education and, for the sake of my parents, find a "nice Jewish girl." Shortly after settling into my off-campus room, my father's sister, Auntie Ester invited me to dinner at her home. I arrived at the appointed hour to discover that I was merely one of two guests. The other was a "nice Jewish girl" my Aunt Ester wanted me to meet-like-love-and-marry (a custom of the 1950's). Though this girl had long, slender fingers and played the clarinet, she suffered from a rather oversized nose that was overshadowed only by two ears that resembled inverted bedpans. Auntie Ester placed this young lady directly across the table from me so that eating my food necessitated casting my eyes upon her (unless I ate with my head turned aside). While my Auntie served and my Uncle Meshy joked, I struggled through the gefilte fish and matzo ball soup, my eyes skipping from ear to ear over the nose, trying to keep from embarrassing myself by staring at one protruberance to the exclusion of the others. My Auntie must have noticed my discomfort because she kept smiling confidently and murmuring "Wait till you taste my brisket" (as though it was a lollipop for a brave little boy).

The aroma annointed my nostrils before the platter even entered the room. A sweetness without sugar; body without weight; succulence without lipids. My head felt light as Auntie dished it onto my plate. It stretched lazily, invitingly, shimmering in its aromatic sauce. "It's a special recipe from my native town of Minsk" I heard her say as I sliced and tasted. Heaven. Heav . . . en. I ate. And as I ate a strange aura seemed to permeate the room. Slowly but perceptively, the ears and the nose that sat across from me began to recede. I swear it. Before my incredulous eyes, they shrank. A tiny button nose. Cute little ears. I chewed; I swallowed; I stared. That young lady was beautiful. I glanced over at my Auntie. She grinned and winked. "Eat your brisket." Lord, how I ate. That beautiful lady is now my wife.

Soy Sauce Stew

• Serves 4

2 pounds beef chuck, in chunks
¼ cup soy sauce
2 cups boiling water
4 carrots, cut into 1-inch pieces
2 cups potatoes, in chunks
2 onions, quartered
1 cup celery, in wide strips
1 diced turnip (optional)
1 clove garlic, through press
   About 1 teaspoon salt (to taste. Be aware of salt in soy sauce)
½ teaspoon Accent
1/8 teaspoon rosemary (optional)
1/8 teaspoon thyme (optional)
1-2 tablespoons cornstarch
2 tablespoons water
1 package frozen green peas or mixed vegetables

Method: Heat meat in soy sauce for 5 minutes. Add boiling water. Simmer until meat is almost tender. Add Accent. Add carrots, potatoes, onions, celery, turnips (if used). Season with garlic, rosemary and thyme. Add salt to taste. Bring meat and vegetables up to boil and cover pot. Reduce heat and simmer for 20 or 30 minutes. Combine 1 or 2 tablespoons cornstarch with 2 tablespoons cold water. Add paste to stew. Bring to boil. Shake pot or stir once or twice. Cook till gravy thickens. Add frozen peas or mixed vegetables. Put stew in casserole. Bake at 400 degrees for 15 minutes.

If desired, top with baking powder biscuits before baking.

Baking Powder Biscuits

2 cups flour
4 teaspoons baking powder
¼ cup shortening
⅔ cup water

Method: Combine dry ingredients. Cut in shortening till flour mixture is crumbly. Add water all at once. Combine with a fork just until dry ingredients are combined and moistened. Roll out ¾-inch thick on floured board. Cut with a biscuit cutter that has been dipped in flour. Place on top of stew in casserole. Bake for 15-20 minutes in 400-degree oven till biscuits are golden.

SUSAN STRASBERG/Sweet and Sour Stuffed Peppers

Kosher Calypso Style

When I was growing up in New York, we had a Jamaican housekeeper who had worked many years for a rabbi. When Ethel first came to our house, all she could cook was kosher, and we didn't keep a kosher household. So here she was, making pot roast we hadn't seen the likes of since my grandmother died. She would say, "That's the way the rabbi did it," with a thick Jamaican accent. She made it sound as if the rabbi had just returned from Mt. Sinai with the decalogue and cookbook in hand.

With that credit, we didn't want to go against anything the rabbi did. Since he always ate in the kitchen, so did we. Ethel was like a waiter in a kosher restaurant. If we left food on the plate, she would stand over us and say, "What's the matter, isn't the food good:" Then she'd taste it. "It's good. Why don't you eat?" she'd say.

There was absolutely no way to diet. If I tried to cut down, she would look at me askance, "Eat a potato. You look too thin!"

Sweet and Sour Stuffed Peppers • Serves 6

1½ pounds ground beef
½ cup water
¼ cup uncooked rice
½ cup chopped onion
1 egg
1 teaspoon salt
    Sprinkle pepper
6 green peppers, tops sliced off and seeds and
    membranes removed

Method: Combine ground beef, ½ cup water, uncooked rice, chopped onion, egg, 1 teaspoon salt and sprinkle pepper. Stuff peppers with meat-rice mixture.

Sauce

2 tablespoons margarine
2 tablespoons flour
    Sprinkle paprika
1 cup water
1 can tomato sauce (1 pound size)

Peel of ½ lemon in strips
½ teaspoon cinnamon, or to taste
½ teaspoon salt, or to taste
  Sugar, salt, cinnamon and lemon juice to taste

Method: Melt margarine. Add 2 tablespoons flour, stirring over low flame until brown. Add a sprinkle of paprika. Remove from heat. Slowly add cup of water, stirring constantly so that sauce is smooth. Add can of tomato sauce. Brıng mixture to boil. Reduce heat to simmer. Add strips of lemon peel, ½ teaspoon (or more) cinnamon and salt to taste. Place stuffed peppers in sauce. Bring back to boil. Then turn heat to simmer, cover and cook on low heat 2 to 3 hours. Correct seasoning to your taste with sugar, salt, lemon juice and cinnamon.

LEON URIS/Braised Lamb Shanks

Exodus

I never graduated from high school in Philadelphia. In fact, I flunked English several times. Fortunately, English and writing have little to do with each other.

I have long had an obsession with Israel and have traveled there many times since 1956. At that time I did extensive research, covering 12,000 miles in a country the size of Connecticut. This trip gave birth to *Exodus*.

The recipe here is one my wife and I discovered on a recent trip to Israel.

Braised Lamb Shanks   • Serves 4

2 tablespoons olive oil
4 lamb shanks, seasoned with salt and pepper
2 onions, diced
2 cloves garlic, crushed
2 carrots, sliced
4 stalks celery, sliced
½ pound mushrooms, sliced
1 19-ounce (#2½) can stewed tomatoes
½ cup red wine
½ cup beef stock
  Salt and pepper to taste
  Bouquet Garni (dried herbs)
½ teaspoon mild curry powder
1 pound string beans, cut in half or whole.
  Rice or noodles

Method: Heat olive oil in heavy iron pot or braising pan. When oil is hot, brown lamb shanks on all sides. Set meat aside and lower heat. Add onions, garlic, carrots and celery and cook over medium heat 5 to 7 minutes. Add and stir mushrooms for 2 minutes. Place meat over vegetables; add stewed tomatoes, wine, stock and seasonings. Cover pot and cook in 325-degree oven 3 hours or until meat is very tender. Add string beans during last 20 minutes of cooking. Serve with rice or noodles.

BOBBY VAN/Kreplach

The Gedempte Dunk

My grandmother used to make gedempte meat. I would wait patiently until all the meat had been eaten, at which time my grandmother would give me the pot with the leftover gravy inside. I'd take the pot with its top on and put it in a brown paper bag. I would then call my friends, and we would meet at the Jewish bakery where we bought a dozen rolls—seeded, bialy and onion. I think it was 10 cents for all the rolls.

Then we would all go to Loew's Burnside in the Bronx and sit with the rolls and the pot and dunk them as we watched the movies. The aroma of gedempte meat filled the theatre. To this day, like one of Pavlov's dogs, I get a hunger pang when I see a marquee. I think they should have gravy and roll concessions in every theatre lobby.

Recently, I went to see a movie in Beverly Hills. On the way I passed a delicatessen, and true to my conditioning, went in to buy a hot potato knish. When the titles started rolling, I bit into the knish. A guy on my left smelled the aroma and tapped me on the shoulder. "What are you eating?" "A potato knish." "Where did you get it?" "Next door." "Save my seat. I'll be right back."

Thirty years pass and nothing changes.

Kreplach • Serves 6

To make the filling, combine:

2 cups cooked meat, minced (cooked beef brisket, rib roast, liver or veal)
1 egg
  Salt and pepper to taste
½ teaspoon onion juice, if desired

To make the noodle dough:

2 cups unsifted all purpose flour
2 eggs
1 tablespoon water
½ teaspoon salt
2-3 quarts boiling salted water

Method: Mound flour in a bowl or on a board and make a "well" in the flour. Add salt, water and eggs in the well. Work and knead the moist mixture into the flour until the mixture is smooth and elastic (one hand is the best equipment for this gooshy job). Roll out the dough as thinly as possible on a well-floured board. Cut dough into 3-inch squares. Place a heaping teaspoon of the meat mixture into each square. Fold the dough making a triangle. Damp the edges of each triangle and press firmly together. Cook in large kettle filled with 2 or 3 quarts boiling salted water for 15 or 20 minutes. (Kreplach will rise to the top when done.)

BARBARA WALTERS/Stuffed Cabbage
Interviewing the Cook

This is my mother's recipe for sweet and sour stuffed cabbage. It is easy to make, smells, I think, delicious when cooking, and tastes likewise. You can make large-sized rolls for a main course or small-sized rolls for an appetizer. My only regret about this recipe is that I don't cook as well as my mother—but then, she doesn't do very good interviews.

Stuffed Cabbage
• Serves 14

3 pounds lean ground chuck
2 teaspoons salt
¾ teaspoon pepper
2 teaspoons celery salt
½ cup catsup
2 eggs
½ cup crushed unsalted crackers
2 heads (2-pound size) green cabbage
6 quarts boiling water
3 cups chopped onion
2 bottles (12-ounce size) chili sauce (2 cups)
1 jar (12-ounce) grape jelly (1 cup)
¼ cup water

Method: In large bowl, combine ground chuck, salt, pepper, celery salt, catsup, eggs and crushed crackers. Mix with hands just until mixture is well combined. Cut out and discard hard center core of cabbage. Place cabbage in large kettle. Pour boiling water over it; let stand until leaves are flexible and can be removed easily from the head—about 5 minutes. (If necessary, return cabbage to hot water to soften inner leaves.) Preheat oven to 375 degrees. Using a ¼-cup measure, scoop up a scant ¼-cup meat mixture. With hands, form into rolls 3 inches long and 1 inch wide, making about 28 rolls in all. Place each meat roll on a drained cabbage leaf; fold top of leaf over meat, then fold sides, and roll up into an oblong. Continue rolling remaining meat rolls and cabbage leaves. In bottom of lightly greased 12 x 11½ x 2¼-inch roasting pan, spread chopped onion evenly. Arrange cabbage rolls in neat rows on top of onion. In 2-quart saucepan, combine chili sauce and grape jelly with ¼ cup water; heat over medium heat, stirring to melt jelly. Pour over cabbage rolls. Cover roasting pan tightly with foil. Bake cabbage rolls 2 hours. Remove foil and brush rolls with sauce. Bake uncovered 40 minutes longer, or until sauce is thick and syrupy and cabbage rolls are glazed. Serve with sauce spooned over rolls.

HENNY YOUNGMAN/Sweet and Sour Ragout

Take My Recipe . . . Please

My wife's cooking is so bad . . . pygmies send their darts to be dipped into her soup to shoot at their enemies.

My mother's cooking was so bad . . . her matzo balls were in demand for hockey pucks.

Mom told me this story: "Shmulke came to school drunk. 'Who did this to you?' the teacher asked. 'Two goyim,' he said. 'Haig & Haig.'"

Essig Fleish with Prunes and Apricots (Sweet and Sour Ragout) • Serves 6-8

3-4 pounds chuck roast (Meat may be left as a
   roast or cut into serving pieces.)
   About 2 teaspoons salt, to taste
   Sprinkle of pepper
2 cloves garlic, put through press or crushed
3 large onions, chopped
2 tablespoons margarine or oil, or rendered fat
   from meat
2 cups water
½ pound prunes and ½ pound dried apricots

(Rinse fruit. Cover with cold water and soak
   several hours.)
   About ½ teaspoon cinnamon, to taste
6 ginger snaps, crushed
½ cup lemon juice or ¼ cup vinegar
   About ¼ cup brown sugar to taste

Method: Wipe meat with damp paper towel. Season meat with 1 teaspoon salt, sprinkle pepper and 1 clove crushed garlic. Using medium high heat, saute chopped onions in 2 tablespoons margarine, oil or fat till onions are golden-brown. Add meat. If left as roast, brown on both sides. If cut into pieces, toss with onions and brown. Add 2 cups water, soaked apricots and prunes and ½ teaspoon cinnamon. Season with second clove of crushed garlic, and salt and pepper to taste. Bring to boil. Reduce heat to simmer. Cover and continue to cook till meat is almost tender (about 2 hours). Combine lemon juice or vinegar, brown sugar and gingersnaps. Add to meat and continue to simmer till meat is tender. Correct seasoning, adding salt, pepper, sugar, cinnamon, lemon juice or vinegar to taste. Serve on cooked barley.

FISH

RUTH JUBELIER GREENWOLD • Fish Cakes
BARRY NEWMAN • Baked Fillet of Sole, Russian
Style
ROBERTA PETERS • Fish Fillets
DR. DAVID REUBEN • Baked Stuffed Fish
SIDNEY SKOLSKY • Baked Fillet of Flounder
PETER YARROW • Martini Tuna Spaghetti

RUTH JUBELIER GREENWOLD/Fish Cakes

Trial by Horseradish

The Chinese laundryman arrived each Friday noon just as my mother's delicious gefilte fish simmered to a "done." Dressed over his ears, his tiny wrinkled face red-rust from Toronto's bitter cold, he looked like a dried lichee nut.

My mother would insist he have lunch. When we came home from school at noon, he would be sitting at the large oil-cloth-covered kitchen table, tears streaming down his face as he ate the gefilte fish, horseradish and challa and talked with my mother—he in Chinese, she in Yiddish. She would always interpret these conversations to us, explaining with a catch in her voice that the "Dremer Mentch" (poor person) was all alone—with no wife or family in this foreign country. How she understood this we never knew, but we did not question its authenticity. To this day I'm not sure whether he cried because of his lonely state or the strength of the freshly grated horseradish.

Fish Cakes • Serves 4
1 pound fillet of fish, ground (mix of fishes best)
2 eggs

2 medium onions, cooked slowly in ½ cup water, seasoned with 1 teaspoon salt and ¼ teaspoon pepper till onions soft and mushy. Cool.
1 slice white bread (challa—egg bread best)
Pinch of sugar
Oil for frying

Method: Put slice of white bread in bottom of wooden chopping bowl. Add cooled, cooked onions and liquid. Chop with single- or double-edged chopper to combine and break up now mushy bread. Add ground fish. Chop to combine. Add eggs, one at a time, as you chop. Season mixture with salt, pepper and sugar. Add enough water to make fish consistency of somewhat loose mashed potatoes. Continue to chop till mixture is light and fluffy (about 5 minutes). Heat large, heavy-bottomed frying pan. Cover bottom with ½ inch vegetable oil. Heat. Make 50-60 fish cakes, using teaspoon as the measure. (Dip spoon in bowl of cold water if necessary. It will keep the fish from sticking to the spoon.) Fry in hot oil. Brown on both sides. Allow to drain on paper towels.

BARRY NEWMAN/Baked Fillet of Sole, Russian Style

My Mother the Taxidermist

My mother is a Jewish taxidermist. Whenever I was near her and I opened my mouth, she would stuff food in it. No one knew I could talk until I was seven. I never got the chance because I was always chewing.

The reason I am bowlegged today is because when I was younger my legs couldn't carry the weight of my body. People were always trying to pick me up to see if I was hollow. I had a cousin who was tall and thin. When we walked down the street, we looked like the Trylon and the Perisphere from the 1939 World's Fair.

Of course, now that I'm starring in a TV show, I'm no longer under the influence of my mother and when I go home for a visit between my *Petrocelli* flimings, I can relax in a chair and watch TV. Subliminally, I see my mother standing in front of me peeling a banana. Since I've seen her do this hundreds of times, I figure it must be a dream. Before I realize what's happening, she's stuffing my mouth with a banana—and I eat it! Do you want to know why? Because it's good for me—right, Ma?

Baked Fillet of Sole, Russian Style

• Serves 5-6

2 pounds fillet of sole
   Butter
½-1 pint sour cream
   Salt, pepper to taste
1-2 tablespoons lemon juice
   About 1 cup corn flakes

Method: Wipe fillets of sole with damp paper towel and arrange a layer of fish in a buttered casserole or baking dish. Season this layer with salt, pepper and part of the lemon juice. Spread a layer of sour cream over the fish and sprinkle the top with cornflakes. Arrange another layer of fish over the first layer. Season and spread with sour cream and cornflakes. Continue layers till all fish is used. Be sure to have sour cream and cornflakes on top. Bake in at 350 degrees 35 to 45 minutes, or until sauce is bubbly and the fish flakes.

ROBERTA PETERS/Fish Fillets

Travels with My Grandmother

Since my mother worked every day as a milliner, my grandmother brought me up. We kept a kosher home while my grandmother was alive. She was an excellent cook and knew the secret of perfect seasoning. Her chopped meat was delicious, even raw. I used to sneak a hunk of raw meat when she wasn't looking. (Grandmother used to wonder why the hamburger shrunk before she cooked it!)

I was an only child and very active. I created mischief and havoc running through the stores when my grandmother and I went shopping. I led her a merry chase between fruit stalls and pickle barrels. To subdue me, she would plunk her hand into the pickle barrel, brine and all, her fingers searching for the longest pickle. When she found it, she would sit me in a corner on top of an orange create, and in the few moments of peace that followed, she would do her shopping and I would do my chewing.

Fish Fillets • Serves 4

8 fillets of sole or blue fish or any other very thin fish fillets

Sauce
¼ cup melted butter
1½ cups soft bread crumbs
¼ cup chopped celery
1 teaspoon grated onion
1 tablespoon chopped parsley
1/8 teaspoon basil
¼ teaspoon salt (to taste)
2 tablespoons butter combined with juice of ½ lemon
Lemon wedges and parsley or watercress for garnish

Method: Butter four individual molds. (You can use 4-inch individual tart molds. The aluminum foil ones will work.) Combine with a fork, melted butter, bread crumbs, chopped celery, grated onion, chopped parsley and sweet basil and salt to taste. Line each mold with two fillets crisscrossed at right angles. Mound a quarter of the bread mixture in the center of the crossed fish fillets. Bring up each fish fillet tip to cover the crumb filling. Place the molds in a pan of hot water. Bake for 30 to 40 minutes in a 350-degree oven. (Fish will turn white and will flake easily.) Unmold on a hot platter. Garnish with lemon wedges, parsley or watercress. Baste fish with sauce or lemon butter.

Any desired seafood sauce may be served with the fish.

DR. DAVID REUBEN/Baked Stuffed Fish

Everything You Wanted to Know about Food—Almost

From a culinary point of view, my childhood left a great deal to be desired. My mother is Scottish and, confidentially, Scottish cooking is not exciting. Their most famous dish is haggis, which is eaten only once a year in Scotland—probably because it is very dull, made mainly of porridge and potatoes and a lot of bread, spiced with salt. It is, however, high in fiber content, a point in its favor. I have long believed that many devastating illnesses are basically the result of our modern, overrefined diet, which is deficient in one indispensable ingredient that is carefully removed during food processing. This missing element in the form of roughage can be added to a daily menu at the cost of two cents a day, and within a few days its beneficial effects can be enjoyed. One of the richest sources of fiber is wheat, specifically the bran portion, or the outermost layer of the wheat kernel. Bran contains the major share of many of wheat's nutrients, including vitamins and minerals. Here is a recipe prepared by my wife, Barbara, that demonstrates how bran can be added to almost anything.

Baked Stuffed Fish

• Serves 8

5- to 7-pound fish (red snapper, lake trout, bluefish, bass, shad, pike, carp, haddock or whitefish)
Salt
Oil or lemon butter for basting
Stuffing (recipe below)

Stuffing

½ cup chopped onion
½ cup mushrooms, cut up
½ cup chopped celery
1 cup (2 sticks) butter
1 cup bran
2 cups bread crumbs
2 teaspoons parsley
½ teaspoon rosemary, tarragon or marjoram
  Salt and pepper to taste
4 tablespoons lemon juice

Method: Saute onions, mushrooms and celery in butter until onions become transparent. Put bran and bread crumbs in a mixing bowl. Add onion mixture, seasonings and lemon juice to bread crumb mixture. Wash fish inside and out with cold water. Dry well and rub inside of fish with a little salt. Spoon in the stuffing, packing lightly. Skewer or sew opening closed. Place fish in greased shallow overproof pan or on greased aluminum foil in a shallow roasting pan. Brush top of fish with oil or lemon butter. Bake at 350 degrees about 50 minutes or until fish flakes easily with a fork. If you brush with lemon butter mixture, baste with it occasionally. A variation is to use fish fillets and put the stuffing between fillets, or roll fillets with stuffing. Brush with oil or lemon butter and bake same as above 30 to 35 minutes or until fish flakes easily when tested with a fork.

SIDNEY SKOLSKY/Baked Fillet of Flounder

Lots of Rolls and a Little Casting

Schwab's Drug Store has been my office and headquarters for 20 years. It's always been a convenient place for film and TV people to meet after a day's shooting, so through the years it's become sort of an urban artists' colony, a private club, a home away from home for hundreds of actors, directors, producers—and me. It's a great communication center, a clearinghouse for information where actors find out from each other what jobs are available and what directors are casting.

My office is on the second level, and by pulling the curtain, I get a view of the whole store below —except the kitchen. And that's fine with me because I can't eat anything if I've seen it prepared. All those fancy preparations at tableside are wasted on me. Just bring me the finished product. Downstairs I always sit in a booth that faces the front of the store so I don't even have to *look* toward the kitchen.

One of my favorite food stories concerns the legendary Diogenes who, when asked the proper time for supper replied: "If you are a rich man, whenever you please; if you are a poor man, whenever you can get it."

Baked Fillet of Flounder • Serves 4

2 large potatoes, sliced
4 medium carrots, sliced
 Margarine or butter
4 medium fillets of flounder, fluke (heavy flounder)
 or sole
 Salt and pepper to taste
 Paprika to taste
 Fresh dill (optional)
1 onion, small and thinly sliced
½ cup milk (approximate)
 Fresh peas, broccoli or asparagus

Method: Parboil potatoes and steam carrots to "oriental" crispness. Put few pats of margarine or butter on bottom of shallow, well-greased baking dish. Place fish fillets on top of margarine. Sprinkle lightly with salt and pepper and generously with paprika. (If fresh dill is available, mince finely and sprinkle on top.) Surround fish with cooked potatoes and carrots and thinly sliced onion (onion can be removed later if desired). Sprinkle potatoes with salt and paprika. Put a few pats of margarine or butter on top of fish. Fill dish with enough milk to come just below top of fish. Bake at 325 degrees 30 minutes. Serve with fresh vegetables (peas, broccoli, asparagus).

PETER YARROW/Martini Tuna Spaghetti

The Culinary Gig

In music, you harmonize, and this recipe is a happy improvisation on three themes.

Martini Tuna Spaghetti   • Serves 3-4

1 sweet onion, chopped
1 7-ounce can tuna
4 tablespoons butter
3 ounces vermouth (¼ cup)
1 ounce gin (2 tablespoons)
  Salt and pepper
  Sweet basil, pinch
1 tablespoon honey
¾ cup heavy cream
½ cup cottage cheese
½ cup Parmesan cheese
½ pound spaghetti, cooked and drained

Method: Saute onion and tuna in butter. Add vermouth and gin; salt and pepper and sweet basil to taste. Simmer about 5 minutes; add honey, heavy cream, cottage cheese and Parmesan cheese. About 2 minutes before serving, add hot cooked, drained spaghetti. Serve with more grated Parmesan cheese and freshly ground pepper.

FOWL

MILTON BERLE • Gefilte Chicken (a la Fish)
JAMES CAAN • Limko
KIRK DOUGLAS • Chicken in Dill Sauce
LORNE GREENE • Chicken in White Wine
DANNY KAYE • Crazy Chicken
HOWARD KOCH • Plum Duckling
HARVEY KORMAN • Waterzooi de Poulet
(Flemish Chicken Stew)
MORLEY MEREDITH • Chicken Supreme
with Prunes

MILTON BERLE/Gefilte Chicken (a la Fish)

But Seriously, Folks

My mother didn't cook much. From the time I was five years old, she devoted herself to taking me around to casting offices. I remember that she once baked a rhubarb pie that was two feet long. When we asked her why she made a two-foot pie, she answered: "I couldn't get any shorter rhubarb."

My father, on the other hand, was the cook of the family. Of German Jewish descent, he lived on 13th Street and First Avenue behind Luchow's Restaurant. As a youth, he could never afford to eat there, so he learned to cook their wonderful dishes himself. His lifelong dream was to own and operate his own restaurant, but it never happened. He had to be content to cook and dream and, when we finally had enough money, to eat many fine dinners at Luchow's.

Gefilte Chicken (a la Fish)   • Serves 4-6

2 onions, sliced
3 carrots, cut up
4 stalks celery
  Bones from four chicken breasts

1 teaspoon salt (approximate)
  Pepper to taste
4 cups water
4 boned chicken breasts
2 medium onions, chopped fine
½ cup cold water
½ cup matzo meal
2 eggs

Method: Put the 2 sliced onions, cut carrots, celery, chicken bones, teaspoon salt, sprinkle pepper and 4 cups water into a large saucepan. Bring mixture to boil, then reduce heat to simmer, cover and cook broth while you prepare chicken. Cut up chicken breasts and chop them well with the 2 chopped onions. Add eggs and continue to chop as you gradually add water and matzo meal alternately. Season mixture with salt and pepper to taste. Remove chicken bones from broth and discard. Bring broth to rolling boil. Dampen hands. Form chicken mixture into balls and drop into the boiling stock. Reduce heat to simmer, cover pot and allow chicken to simmer an hour or so.

JAMES CAAN/Limko

A Souper Blooper

It was my very first bachelor pad and my parents came over to visit me. They scanned the apartment with grave doubts. Their actor son was living alone. Surely he'll starve to death.

To allay any fears of my not being able to cope with the art of cooking, I planned to serve a meal, starting with chicken soup.

The pot had been boiling for over an hour. I sat my parents at the table and carefully served my creation, watching their faces with great anticipation. They tasted the soup. No one spoke.

"Okay," I said. "What's wrong?"

My mother got up and went to the pot in the kitchen, pulled the chicken from the pot and proceeded, with a knife, to clean out the arteries, veins, gall bladder, gizzard . . .

My father looked at my mother. "At least he remembered to throw away the wrapping paper!"

Limko
• Serves 4-5

1 green pepper, chopped
2 onions, chopped
½ pound mushrooms, sliced
4 stalks celery, sliced
¼ cup margarine
1 clove garlic, put through garlic press
1 teaspoon salt
1 tablespoon paprika
3 carrots, sliced
4 whole tomatoes, sliced
¼ cup dry red wine
1 6-ounce package of dry roasted peanuts
1 frying chicken, cut up and cooked 45 minutes in 1½ cups water and 2 teaspoons salt.

Method: Saute chopped green pepper, chopped onions, sliced mushrooms and celery in ¼ cup margarine until onion wilts. Add crushed garlic, 1 teaspoon salt, paprika, sliced carrots, tomatoes and wine. Bring to boil. Reduce heat to simmer and cook 15 minutes or until carrot slices are tender. Combine vegetables mixture with chicken and broth. Cook 30 minutes longer. Correct seasoning. Add peanuts.

KIRK DOUGLAS/Chicken in Dill Sauce

The Heart of the Matter

When I reflect on my youth, I find it difficult to relate to the skinny kid who was so poor that even chicken soup was a rarity to him. While other kids dreamed of baseballs or footballs, I dreamed of chicken soup.

In my early years in Hollywood, I struggled and literally starved. My mother knew of my desire to act, but she was also aware of my desire to eat. She knew I hadn't been successful, and it greatly distressed her. Finally, my big break came. I was signed to a three-picture deal with a major studio. I couldn't wait to get to a phone to tell my mother to stop worrying. When I heard her voice on the other end, I screamed, "Ma, I just signed to star in three motion pictures!"

There was a slight pause on the other end. Then came the reply, "That's nice, but are you eating enough?"

Chicken in Dill Sauce • Serves 3-4

1 frying chicken, cut up
   Salt and pepper
2 or 3 tablespoons margarine
4 scallions, chopped
3 peeled tomatoes, chopped (To.peel: blanch tomatoes by first dipping in boiling water for a minute or two, then dip in cold water and skin will peel readily.)
   Chopped dill (to taste)
½ cup sherry
½ pint pareve sour cream substitute

Method: Wipe chicken parts with damp paper towels. Season chicken with salt and pepper and brown in margarine. During last 5 minutes of browning, add scallions. Cook until greens wilt and white stems turn golden. Add tomatoes, dill and sherry. Cover and cook 1 hour in 325-degree oven or electric fry pan. Remove chicken. Add sour cream substitute to pan. Combine. (Do not allow to boil.) Put chicken back into sauce and heat below the boil for 10 minutes. Don't let sauce boil, or it will curdle.)

LORNE GREENE/Chicken in White Wine

The Chocolate Cake Caper

When I was a boy, one night after a movie a friend and I went back to my house. It was about 10:30, and my parents weren't home yet. We went into the kitchen and were delighted to see a chocolate cake. I took out a quart of milk and cut a piece of the cake, which was in an oblong pan about two feet long and one foot wide. We finished the milk and our cake. Being young, healthy and hungry, we went back for more milk and more cake. We consumed that, and went back for more.

Two and a half quarts of milk and three-quarters of a chocolate cake later, my parents came home. My mother went into the kitchen and gave a yell. "What's the matter, Mom?" I asked. She didn't answer me. There she sat, her eyes fixed on the single remaining slice, now an inadequate contribution for the next morning's Hadassah tea. She stayed up until four in the morning baking another cake. To this day I can't look at a chocolate cake without feeling guilty.

Chicken in White Wine   • Serves 4-6

4 chicken breasts
4 chicken legs
2 onions, sliced
2 cups dry white wine
   Margarine
   Salt and pepper (if desired)
   Rice

Method: Skin chicken parts and place in large Pyrex dish. Arrange sliced onions on chicken. Pour wine over chicken and onions. Dot with margarine; salt sparingly and add pepper if desired. Bake at 350 degrees 45 minutes. Remove and place under broiler to brown chicken parts. Keep turning chicken until well browned. Serve with rice.

DANNY KAYE/Crazy Chicken

First Things First

As a young man, I spent two years in the Orient traveling in a review called "La Vie Paris." I survived scorpions, typhoons and flying cockroaches and emerged with many lessons in stage poise. The Oriental stagehands were absolutely unpredictable. I never knew if a prop or a piece of furniture would be there on cue, and many times I had to improvise and be funny without props.

The Japanese consider it bad manners to applaud during a show, and they sit there deadpan. We had to teach them how to applaud. The Chinese of course, giggle behind their hands a lot. Neither trait exactly bolsters the fragil ego of a performer.

I also emerged with a love of Chinese cooking whose technique is based on the historical stortage of fuel. Food is prepared in tiny pieces in a quick, stir-fried manner because that is how long the gathered twigs would burn.

My father had a great sense of timing. When I returned home after my Far Eastern tour, I burst excitedly into the house. Pop looked up and said, "Hello, son, there's milk in the icebox."

Crazy Chicken • Serves 8

1½ cups skinned, boned chicken cut in ½-inch cubes
1 egg white
4 tablespoons peanut, corn or other vegetable oil
1 tablespoon cornstarch
½ cup thinly sliced water chestnuts
10 litchi nuts, cut into quarters
1 tablespoon dry sherry or shao hsing Chinese wine
1 tablespoon light soy sauce
½ teaspoon sambal oelik (Indonesian hot chili)
  Salt to taste
½ teaspoon sugar
½ cup roasted peanuts crushed

Method: Combine chicken, egg white, 1 tablespoon oil and cornstarch. Mix well with fingers. Refrigerate 30 minutes. Heat remaining 3 tablespoons oil in a wok or skillet and add chicken, stirring rapidly just to separate pieces. Drain chicken, reserving 2 tablespoons oil for wok. Add chicken; stir quickly 30 seconds. Add water chestnuts and litchis; stir to blend. Add wine, soy sauce, sambal oelik, salt and sugar; stir and toss quickly. Add peanuts; toss quickly and serve.

HOWARD KOCH/Plum Duckling

A Touch of Class

My mother, the daughter of a cantor rabbi and the daughter-in-law of a cantor rabbi, was a gas. She wore spike heels, cut her hair in a boyish bob, and went to tea dances. She had style. Her parents pampered her all her life and my father did the same in their married life.

One day, late in the afternoon, my father had not returned with the houseboy who doubled as driver and cook. My mother called all around New York—every restaurant, club and office—but they were not to be found. Frantically, she eyed the uncooked chicken that waited in the refrigerator, and a fear that had haunted her all her life—that she would have to take off her white gloves and prepare food—was finally happening.

But her family must be fed. Where should she start? Being a fastidious woman, she took out a brush, and a bar of soap, and scrubbed the poor chicken with vigor. Then she found a pan, put the chicken in, slopped a pound of margarine on the unsuspecting bird and slammed it into the oven.

Fighting off the vapors, she retired to her chambers, with her heart beating furiously.

Finally the family sat down to eat.

It was the best chicken we ever had.

When you've got it, you've got it!

Plum Duckling   • Serves 3-4

4½ to 5-pound duckling
    Salt and pepper
1 onion, chopped fine
2 tablespoons parsley, chopped fine
2 tablespoons margarine
1 clove garlic, put through press (optional)
1 cup long grain rice, cooked
1 teaspoon curry powder
¼ teaspoon allspice
1 tablespoon brown sugar
    Salt to taste
    Jar of plum jam (6 ounces)
¼ cup Madeira wine
½ teaspoon freshly grated ginger root (or use ¼ teaspoon of powdered ginger)
    Sprinkle of grated nutmeg

Method: Make stuffing by sauteeing onion and parsley in margarine until onion becomes slightly golden. Remove from heat and add garlic (if used), cooked rice, curry powder, allspice, brown sugar and salt to taste. Wash and dry duckling. Remove excess fat from around neck and cavity. Season duckling inside and out with salt and pepper before stuffing lightly with the rice dressing. Sew or truss closed and skewer wings to sides of duck. Set duckling, breast down, on rack in shallow pan and bake in 375-degree oven 45 minutes to brown and render some of the fat. Pour excess fat from pan. Turn duckling breast side up. Reduce oven temperature to 325 degrees and continue to roast 2 to 2½ hours (till tender). Combine plum jam, wine, ginger and nutmeg. Pour excess fat out of pan. Baste duckling on all sides with plum sauce. Allow duckling to bake 20 to 30 minutes longer. Serve with extra sauce in a sauceboat.

Easiest way to serve is to cut duckling into quarters using poultry shears.

HARVEY KORMAN/Waterzooi de Poulet

Lost in the Translation

We first tasted waterzooi while traveling in Belgium some years ago with our friends, Sheila and Ron Clark. He is the comedy writer.

Not long after we returned home, my wife, Donna labored all day long, and finally we were breathlessly at the table, anticipating that thick, flavorful concoction, only to behold and taste a rather thin, treacly kind of watery soup. We all sat there disappointed and bewildered, afraid to say anything, when Ron broke the silence. "This is quite different from the waterzooi in Belgium, isn't it? It seems to have a lot less zooi and a lot more water."

Waterzooi de Poulet
(Flemish Chicken Stew)

• Serves 4-6

8 chicken parts (breasts and thighs)
  Salt and pepper to taste
3 cloves garlic put through press, or chopped
3 tablespoons margarine
3 tablespoons oil
2 onions, chopped
2 leeks, white part only, chopped
1 stalk celery (green top too), chopped
3 cups chicken broth
  Monosodium glutamate, if desired
1 celery root, peeled and cut into 1-inch cubes
4 carrots, sliced
12 small white boiling onions
6 small potatoes, peeled, or 3 large potatoes,
  peeled and cut into halves
½ pound or more small whole mushrooms

Method: Wipe chicken parts with damp paper towels. Season with salt, pepper and 2 cloves crushed garlic. Heat margarine and oil in a large saucepan, using medium high heat, and brown seasoned chicken parts in hot fat. Remove chicken and pour off excess fat. Put chopped onion, leek, celery stalk and third clove of crushed garlic into saucepan. Add 3 cups chicken broth. Heat to boiling. Add browned chicken parts to stock and vegetables. Season with salt and monosodium glutamate. Lower heat, cover and simmer 30 minutes. Add celery root cubes, carrot slices, boiling onions, potatoes and mushrooms. Bring broth back to boil. Reduce heat to simmer and cover, cooking till potatoes, carrots and celery root are tender (about 25 minutes). Correct seasoning with salt and pepper. Spoon excess fat off top of broth is necessary; serve in large soup bowls.

Celery root turns black when exposed to air, so keep it covered with water if you peel it before you are ready to add it to the stew.

MORLEY MEREDITH/Chicken Supreme with Prunes

Stroganoff Anonymous

About twice a year, my wife and I have a big dinner party for some of my Metropolitan Opera colleagues. On one such occasion, we found ourselves momentarily in a stew when the bartender approached Jerome Hines to ask for his drink order. Jerry replied "Club soda, please." Then we realized that when we planned the menu we had completely forgotten that the famous basso is a total teetotaler.

That evening we were serving: beef stroganoff cooked in champagne, barley casserole marinated in rum, and fruit compote baked in Grand Marnier! My wife offered to make Jerome a steak, but he replied it wasn't necessary. "After all that cooking, I'm sure it's passed through purgatory and is now cleansed and diffused of all its alcoholic content." He ate with relish and even took seconds, but I do think I saw him put the sauce to the side.

Chicken Supreme with Prunes • Serves 6-8

4 large chicken breasts
16 pitted prunes (more for garnish is desired)
½ cup or more dark rum (enough to cover prunes)
  Salt and pepper to taste
  Spice mixture (recipe below)
  Cling peach halves (optional)
  Watercress for garnish

Spice Mixture

1 large onion, coarsely chopped
1 green pepper, seeded and chopped
1 tomato, peeled, seeded and chopped
1 red or green chile pepper, seeded and chopped
3 garlic cloves, chopped
2 tablespoons curry powder
1 tablespoon fresh coriander (cilantro) leaves
1 teaspoon oregano
½ teaspoon cumin seed

Method: Have butcher bone and skin chicken breasts and split them in half. Flatten each "supreme" with a small mallet. Soak prunes for at least 2 hours in enough rum to cover. In blender, combine all ingredients of spice mixture, blend, scraping down the sides, until it is a thick puree. Season each supreme with salt and pepper and place two prunes on each one. Then roll, completely enclosing the filling. Use toothpicks to hold together. Coat the supreme with the spice mixture. Place pieces in large dish or pan for baking, cover and refrigerate overnight. Bake the supremes at 350 degrees about 45 minutes or until tender. Arrange on platter and garnish with watercress. If desired, you may also use cling peach halves and additional rum-soaked prunes for garnish.

VEGETABLES AND SIDE DISHES

MARTY ALLEN • Barley Casserole
SHELLEY BERMAN • Knishes
HERB ALPERT • Vegetable Savory Loaf
JOEY BISHOP • Verenikas (Pirogen)
NORM CROSBY • Noodle Pudding
RABBI JEROME CUTLER • Cauliflower Latkes
SAMMY DAVIS, JR. • Greens (Collard)
EYDIE GORME • Spinach Souffle
STANLEY MYRON HANDELMAN • Tsimis (Honey
                                        Carrots)
ARTHUR HILLER • Lazy Cheese Knishes
SAM JAFFE • Tsimis Naheet (Chick Peas)
ARTE JOHNSON • Ratatouille
ROBERT KLEIN • Hungarian Potatoes
JACK KLUGMAN • Kasha Varnishka
MICHELE LEE • Stuffed Tomatoes
WALTER MATTHAU • Kasha (Groats)
NEHEMIAH PERSOFF • Mushrooms and Potatoes
DON RICKLES • Kasha
MRS. RICHARD TUCKER • Noodle Pudding

MARTY ALLEN/Barley Casserole

The Kids Gave My Mother an "A"

I grew up in Pittsburgh, and we lived near Taylor Allderdice High School where I went. I was a pretty good student and never played hooky, but many of my friends did. Because we lived so near the school, sometimes my friends would cut a class they didn't like and spend the rest of the day at my house. My mother, who made *me* go to school, would feel sorry for those hooky players and would cook and bake for them.

When I got home from school, I sometimes found ten or fifteen of my friends there playing games and eating. All I got were the leftovers.

As word got around, more and more kids started playing hooky and going to my house for food. It got so that I could hardly wait for the school bell to ring at the end of the day so I could run home and be with my buddies.

This recipe is my mother's and was loved by everybody—especially the truant officer who ate first and then took the kids in.

Barley Casserole • Serves 4-5

1 large onion, chopped
½ cup mushrooms, sliced
5 tablespoons margarine
1 cup egg barley
2 cups chicken soup
Salt to taste

Method: Saute onion and mushrooms in margarine. Add barley. Fry to a golden brown. Pour into greased casserole, cover with 1 cup of soup, add salt to taste and bake 1 hour at 350 degrees. Add other cup of soup, return to oven and bake an additional 15 minutes.

HERB ALPERT/Vegetable Savory Loaf

Change of Menu

Every Friday night at our house the traditional meal was always the same: chopped liver, boiled chicken, chicken soup, apple sauce and challah. After the meal, we retired into the sitting room where the piano was. My father would take out his mandolin, which he played by ear, my mother, her violin, my sister Mimi sat at the piano, David, my brother, took out his skins, and I unpacked my horn. We would play a variety of contemporary and Yiddish songs.

Finally, after having the same menu for many, many months, we approached my mother tactfully.

"Ma, do you notice how our selections change after each Friday night meal?" She nodded yes. "Well, ma, do you think you could also vary the meal on Friday night?" She didn't answer.

When next Friday came, we waited anxiously to see if there was going to be any innovation on Mother's part. An air of expectancy filled the room as we sat at the table. The first dish was . . . chopped liver . . . again. Being careful not to show our disappointment, we ate it up.

My mother then collected the dishes. "And now," she announced, "the piece de resistance." She ran into the kitchen.

I could feel the tension rising. The flavor buds in my mouth were ready for anything. I picked up my horn and gave a "da da ta ta."

The door opened and momma stood there holding the dish.

My father spoke first. "But it's chicken," he said, crestfallen.

"Yes," Momma replied, "but it's fried."

Vegetable Savory Loaf   • Serves 4-6

1 tablespoon butter, melted
1 tablespoon soy flour
¼ cup cream
2 eggs
1½ cups cooked, cut asparagus
1 small chopped onion
1 green pepper, chopped
1 large tomato, peeled and chopped
6 mushrooms, sliced

2 zucchini, sliced
1½ cups grated cheddar cheese
½ teaspoon vegetized salt, to taste

Method: Combine butter and flour. Add cream, stirring to make a smooth sauce. Beat eggs and add to creamy mixture. Combine cooked, cut asparagus, chopped onion, green pepper, tomato, mushrooms and sliced zucchini. Add grated cheddar cheese to vegetables. Combine vegetable-cheese mixture with the cream sauce. Season with salt. Bake in 1-quart casserole (or a long pan) in medium (325-350-degree) oven 45 minutes to 1 hour.

SHELLEY BERMAN/Knishes

Rollerball—Starring Shelley Berman

My fondest memory is when my grandmother would mash potatoes. I grew up loving mashed potatoes with chicken schmaltz. I would stand next to the stove like a little puppy dog because I knew that as soon as the potatoes were properly mashed, my grandmother would take a little handful, roll it into a little ball and pop it into my mouth. Even today when I sit down and have mashed potatoes—when nobody is looking—I take a little handful, roll it into a ball and pop it into my mouth.

When you get caught, how do you explain it? What can you reply when your wife and children look at you and say, "Why are you rolling the potatoes into a ball?" They just don't understand.

Knishes • Serves 8

2 cups all-purpose flour
¾ cup shortening
2 teaspoons baking powder
¾ teaspoons salt
1 egg
½ cup water
   Few teaspoons matzo meal
   Chicken fat (schmaltz) at a spreadable room temperature

Method: Combine flour, baking powder and salt. Cut shortening into dry ingredients, using a pastry cutter (or your fingers) until mixture is crumbly. Combine egg and water. Pour into the flour-shortening mixture, stirring till all is combined. Cut mixture in two. Shape into balls and chill overnight in two oiled saucers. Cover with wax paper. (The dough will be sticky before chilling.)

Filling

1½ pounds liver, sauteed or baked (don't overcook)
4 potatoes, cooked, drained and mashed
2 large onions, chopped and sauteed till golden
   brown in 2 tablespoons chicken fat
   Grieben (chicken cracklings)
   Salt, pepper to taste

Method: Put cooked liver and onions through a grinder. Add ground liver and onions to mashed potatoes. Season to taste with chicken fat, salt, pepper and grieben. Cool.

When Ready to Bake: Remove dough from refrigerator and allow to sit at room temperature for ½ hour before rolling out on a floured board. Roll each ball, one at a time, in a long, thin rectangle. Place part of filling down length of rolled-out sheet of dough. Roll as for a jelly roll. Using a pastry brush, brush filled roll with chicken schmaltz. Then sprinkle with matzo meal or bread crumbs. Cut roll into 2-inch pieces, using the heel of your hand— karate-chop style. Flatten slightly like a puff. Take each puff end, stand it on end, thus making the end the top. Place knishes on an oiled baking pan, allowing a small space between each one. Baste with schmaltz. Bake in 400-degree oven for 10 minutes. Rduce heat to 375 degrees and bake for 15 minutes longer (till golden).

JOEY BISHOP/Verenikas (Pirogen)

Have Pirogen, Will Travel

The thing that I remember best about my childhood is Friday. Every Friday when I came home from school, there were papers on the linoleum floor in the kitchen, which my mother had just washed.

We didn't stay in the kitchen or house too long because Friday meant chicken, and my mother would be singeing its feathers off over the gas range. When you tiptoed in (otherwise you would upset the cake in the oven), first you smelled the soap that cleaned the floor, but when you hit the kitchen . . . I think in those days I was already wishing Colonel Sanders would break a leg.

We kept a strictly kosher house. As a matter of fact, when I appeared in a nightclub, my mother and father would come and bring a fork, a plate, and a can of Bumblebee salmon for dinner.

I was the youngest of five, and I remember my mother hitting me because I wasn't eating. But one dish my mother made, pirogen, was my favorite. Years later, whenever I was working in the nightclubs in Vegas or in New York, whoever came from Philadelphia brought me some from my mother. Whenever a maitre d' smelled the heavenly aroma of pirogen coming from a paper bag in the hand of someone waiting to be seated, he would say, "And how is Philadelphia?" They would always wonder how the maitre d' knew they were from Philadelphia.

Verenikas (Pirogen)
• Serves 6-8

2 cups all-purpose flour
2 eggs
½ teaspoon salt
   About 1 tablespoon water
   Filling (recipe below)
   Boiling salted water

Method for Dough: Place flour on a board in a mound. Make a well in the flour. Put eggs, salt and water into the well. Work the eggs, water and salt into the flour (best equipment, your hands) and knead dough until it is smooth and stretches readily. Roll dough out as thin as possible. Cut into 3-inch circles and fill with filling, next page.

Filling

2 cups mashed potatoes (made with cooked, well-drained potatoes)
½ cup chopped onions sauteed in 2 tablespoons chicken fat
2 hard-boiled eggs, chopped
Grieben (cracklings) made by rendering chicken fat and browning and crisping chicken skin bits in the melting fat (optional). (The chicken bits are the grieben.)
2 quarts water
Salt, pepper to taste
More chicken fat (optional)

Method for Filling: Combine mashed potatoes with sauteed onions, chopped hard-boiled eggs and 1 or 2 tablespoons grivenes (if desired). Season with salt and pepper. Place a spoonful of the mashed potato mixture on each circle of dough. Dampen edge of half the circle with a little water. Enclose mashed potatoes by folding circle in half. Pinch edges together. Cook pirogen in vigorously boiling salted water until pirogen float to the top (takes about 10 minutes). Drain and serve with more chicken schmaltz and a sprinkle of grieben if you dare!

Serve with barrel of seltzer.

NORM CROSBY/Noodle Pudding

A Blintz-Krieg

My grandmother was one of the all-time best cheese blintz makers. She made perfectly shaped, golden brown, semi-crisp delights that smelled magnificent. Because of the intense heat in the kitchen, she would bake with the windows opened.

The kids in our old neighborhood would camp outside her window waiting for the aroma to drift by their sensitive noses and as soon as the first whiff wafted by, they would make a beeline for the kitchen.

Nonchalantly, my friends, my family and I would pass by the oven and sample a blintz . . . or two. My grandmother kept on grinding out the blintzes, unmindful of the "bread line" in her kitchen. Then, after hours of squeezing and rolling, she would turn from the stove in amazement and find the large trays absolutely bare.

"Where did all the blintzes disappear to?" she would ask.

But, grandmother, smart old sleuth that she was, knew. She never seemed to mind.

Noodle Pudding • Serves 4

2 eggs
1 carton whipped cream cheese (4 ounce)
½ teaspoon salt
½ cup milk
½ cup sugar
½ cup raisins
¼ teaspoon cinnamon
8 ounces flat noodles, cooked and drained

Method: Beat eggs and add cream cheese, salt, pepper, milk, sugar, raisins and cinnamon. Gently fold in noodles. Pour into buttered 1-quart casserole. Bake 1 hour in 325-degree oven.

RABBI JEROME CUTLER/Cauliflower Latkes

That's Show Biz

Tuesday was dish night at the Carroll Theatre in Crown Heights, Brooklyn. As an incentive to drive people away from Uncle Miltie and the TV set, the management gave away white dishes with a silver edge on the border. The first Tuesday of the month a dinner plate was given, the second, a soup plate, the third a cup and the fourth a saucer.

Since the dishes were given upon entry to the theatre, by the time the show ended people forgot they were on their laps. Then, throughout the theatre you heard a cacophony of dishes breaking when people stood up—followed by a loud "OY VEY IS MIR." Now the poor woman would have to come back the third Tuesday of next month to get her cup.

When the Carroll Theatre stopped giving out dishes there was wholesale trading between the women who were a few saucers or a main dish or two short. Everyone traded, for there wasn't one woman who, during the time of giving out dishes, didn't at one time or another give out with an "OY VEY IS MIR."

Cauliflower Latkes

1 head cooked cauliflower
1 small onion
1 small bunch parsley
½ cup bread crumbs
1 well-beaten egg
  Cornflake crumbs
  Shortening

Method: Finely chop 1 cooked, cold cauliflower. Mix in 1 small, finely chopped onion, 1 small bunch of parsley, chopped fine, ½ cup bread crumbs and 1 well-beaten egg. Mix together well and mold into croquette forms, dip in cornflake crumbs and fry in hot shortening until light brown.

SAMMY DAVIS, JR./Greens (Collard)

My Way

Food has never really been that important to me, as you can tell by my hulking hundred and fifteen frame—soaking wet. For me, it has always been a question of eating for survival or for purely social reasons. When I find myself getting hungry, which is normally at very odd hours in the morning, I generally pick myself up from bed and very quietly, so as not to disturb Altovise, tiptoe out of the room. As soon as I pass the threshold, I hear a voice from beneath the blankets, "The chicken soup is in the big pot, and the vegetable soup in the little one."

Then I trot into the kitchen and put the pot of my choice on the stove. Sometimes, when I desire a real gourmet treat, I mix the two soups together— "Ain't no soul food ever tasted like that!" In a way, eating kosher food comes close to soul food for me, and since I've been in show business, I've eaten more kosher dishes than black-eyed peas.

Greens (Collard)   • Serves 4

6 bunches of collard greens
4 pounds flanken
1 green pepper, diced
2 onions, diced
 Pinch of sugar
 Pinch of baking soda
4 whole dry red peppers
 Salt and pepper to taste

Method: Cook flanken in water to cover for about 3 hours, until meat falls off bones. Reserve meat. Wash greens 5 or 6 times in salt water, break them up in pieces and cook them in broth from the flanken. Then add peppers, onion, sugar, soda, red pepper. Cook for 45 minutes.

Add meat or serve it separately with strong white horseradish and cornbread. Dunk bread into soup.

EYDIE GORME/Spinach Souffle

At the Captain's Table

When Steve and I went on tour to Europe, we took my mother. We booked first-class passage on the *Queen Mary*; outside cabins, dinner at the captain's table, the best-placed deck chairs. The works.

At dinner our first night out, there was great pomp and circumstance, with a display of waiters and busboys catering to our every wish. In the midst of this gala array of English hospitality, my mother started to laugh. At first the laughter was subdued, but it escalated with every royal gesture shown by our hosts. Soon her laughter became contagious, and everyone at the table joined in although I must admit Steve's and mine was more nervous than joyful.

Finally, when someone asked, "Why are you laughing?" she answered with tears streaming down her cheeks: "I'm sorry, I was comparing this to a previous crossing—when I came steerage on a freighter from Turkey. And you know something? This way's better. Pass the caviar."

Spinach Souffle   • Serves 10-12

12 cups fresh spinach, chopped fine (equals 3 bunches or 2¼ pounds)
8 eggs
2 medium-size boiled potatoes, grated, or ¼ cup matzo meal
4 ounces grated Kaskaval cheese
8 ounces small curd cottage, pot or hoop cheese
2 teaspoons salt
¼ cup oil

Method: In a large bowl, mix spinach, eggs, potatoes or matzo meal, cheeses and salt. In a 9 x 14 baking pan, pour all of the oil, then the spinach mixture. Bake at 350 degrees approximately 1 hour until golden brown and firm. Allow to cool slightly and cut into serving size squares.

This dish freezes well. Can be reheated at 350 degrees.

STANLEY MYRON HANDELMAN/Tsimis (Honey Carrots)

Recycled

My wife used to cook a gourmet meal when she prepared squab. The procedure was most complicated. She would wrap the squab in cheesecloth and marinate it in lemon juice, garlic and margarine for two days. Then she would put it in an earthenware pot over a slow flame for about eight hours. After simmering, she would take this delicious dish and finally present it. And if you closed your eyes, you'd swear it was fried chicken.

I had an uncle who felt the best parts of the food are thrown out—like celery leaves, orange rinds, egg shells, and tea bags. People, he claimed, ate the rest and it had no food value. So he sold a tonic to make up for all the loss and I tried it. To me, it tasted just like something you throw down the drain.

Tsimis (Honey Carrots)   • Serves 4

6 or 8 carrots, sliced diagonally (French-fry cutter makes them pretty)

½ cup boiling water or ½ cup orange juice
  Salt, pepper to taste
2-3 tablespoons butter or margarine
½ teaspoon dry mustard
4 tablespoons honey or brown sugar
  Squeeze of lemon juice
1 or 2 tablespoons green onion tops, or chives, diced fine
½ cup orange juice

Method: Cook carrots in boiling water, covered, till carrots are almost tender. Remove cover and continue to cook rapidly till all excess water is evaporated. Season with salt, pepper, margarine or butter, mustard and honey and lemon juice. Cook over low heat, spooning sauce over carrots till they are glazed. When ready to serve, sprinkle chopped green onions or chives over carrots.

If you prefer orange-flavored carrots, cook carrots in orange juice till tender. Reduce liquid. Then season with grated orange peel, brown sugar, butter or margarine, salt and pepper to taste.

ARTHUR HILLER/Lazy Cheese Knishes

Roman Holiday

Have you tried to prepare an American Thanksgiving dinner in Rome? Don't! Yams and cranberries are nonexistent. While I was directing *Man of La Mancha*, my wife, Gwennie, finally convinced a greengrocer on the Via del Croce to import them for her so we could introduce Peter O'Toole and Sophia Loren to this American tradition. Mistake! Neither of them could stand the sweet taste of yams or the cranberries. So, as the rest of us turkeyed, Peter and Sophia delighted in Gwennie's refrigerated supply of chopped chicken liver and lazy cheese knishes.

Lazy Cheese Knishes • Serves 4

Requires overnight preparation.

1 cup white flour
¼ pound butter
1 carton or ½ pound cottage cheese
  Filling (recipe below)

Method for Dough: Combine flour and butter. Toss it lightly with your finger or use a pastry blender. Add cheese and combine. Chill overnight.

Filling

(Prepare the next day)
6 ounces cottage cheese, drained (or use farmer-style cheese)
1 egg
  Pinch of salt
  Also, you may use a little sugar and cinnamon if you desire a sweeter taste

Method for Filling: Combine cottage cheese, eggs and salt and sugar and cinnamon if used. Roll dough on floured board to a sheet about 1/8-inch thick. Cut out round shapes about 1½-inch in diameter, or triangular shapes of similar size. Place a small amount of cheese in center of each shape, dampen edge of dough with water and pinch dough together on all sides, enclosing cheese. Bake about 15 minutes at 425 degrees.

SAM JAFFE/Tsimis Naheet (Chick Peas)

Tsimis, Tsimis, Tsimis

The number three has always been a digit of good fortune. Dream something good three times in a row, it will come true. Rub a wedding ring three times on the eye, it will cure a stye. Turn it around three times, make a wish, and it will happen.

It is an omen of good luck, if one sneezes three times. The Italians say any trinity is lucky. For me, the trinity I find lucky are the three ingredients chick peas, rice and honey. The reason, my dear friends, is because those ingredients comprise a most sovereign and palatable dish called "tsimis naheet."

The expression, "Make yourself a tsimis of it," is a euphemism for "So rave about it," and a good tsimis is something one can really rave about—and be lucky to eat!

Tsimis Naheet (Chick Peas)   • Serves 6

½ **pound chick peas,**
1 cup rice
  Honey to taste
  Butter to taste
  Salt to taste

Method: Soak chick peas overnight in water. Drain chick peas, cover completely with boiling salted water and cook covered till tender (about 35 minutes). Cook 1 cup rice in 2 cups salted water, covered, till all water is absorbed and rice is tender. Add cooked rice to the tender chick peas. Season with salt, honey and butter to taste. Allow to simmer to combine flavors before serving.

ARTE JOHNSON/Ratatouille

Grandpa's Big Blast

We lived in the country in Michigan, and at the end of the season the women used to can in Mason jars. You never bought canned goods; you made your own.

One afternoon the women were boiling the jars on top of the coal-burning stove to sterilize them. Under the stove there was an open spill area. On this particular day, they were cooking string beans and one of the girls saw a mouse in that little area. After all, it was a farm. She let out piercing shrieks for my grandfather.

He came with his shotgun, mad at this mouse because it had made him come in all the way from the back of the farm. He stepped through the door, spotted the intruder, took careful aim, and blasted away.

Needless to say, the mouse got away. My grandfather, however, succeeded in breaking every jar on the stove.

The green beans exploded and were hanging from the ceiling like stalactites for weeks.

Ratatouille   • Serves 4-6

2 eggplants, peeled, sliced lengthwise
1 large onion, chopped
¼ pound margarine
1 green pepper, chopped
¼ pound mushrooms, sliced
⅔ cup safflower oil
4 zucchini, sliced
2 tomatoes, peeled and chopped
  Parmesan cheese
½ can black olives, pitted
  Salt and pepper to taste
2 cloves garlic, crushed

Method: Cover eggplant slices with salted water. Soak 30 minutes. Drain. Saute onion in margarine until translucent. Add green peppers and mushrooms; saute mushrooms until brown. Season with salt and pepper. In separate pan, brown eggplant slices in oil and add zucchini. Stir fry 2 minutes. Add crushed garlic. Fill large casserole with alternate layers of eggplant, sauteed mixture, zucchini and diced tomatoes. Sprinkle top with cheese and olives. Bake in 350-degree oven 45 minutes.

ROBERT KLEIN/Hungarian Potatoes

Ma and Pa-prika

The kitchen in our apartment was very small. There were four of us—my mother, my father, my sister and I. My mother could reach any point in the kitchen from her chair. It was sort of a command post.

All four of my grandparents are Hungarian, so the cooking influence in the house was Jewish Hungarian, which means no sour cream in the goulash. But there was a tremendous paprika onslaught. Paprika has a lot of bark, but no bite; it's truly a misleading condiment. My mother used to buy it in the largest possible commercial package—a pound size. She'd always have about two or three packages going at the same time.

It was only after I had left home and gone to school for four years that I realized that paprika is not like plasma and it is possible to live a full, productive life without it.

My mother never kept a "Biblical" kosher home, but we didn't have milk or butter on the table with meat. It was a subliminal no-no.

A few older members of my family upheld the Jewish traditions, but my father used to add a note of levity to the Seder by answering the question, "Why is this night different from all other nights?" by saying, "Because yesterday was Thursday and today is Friday."

Hungarian Potatoes • Serves 2-3

4 medium potatoes
2 medium onions, chopped fine
2 tablespoons shortening (or more, to taste)
　Salt and pepper to taste
　Paprika

Method: Cook potatoes, drain and mash. Saute chopped onions in 2 tablespoons shortening till browned. Add salt and pepper to taste and be generous with the paprika. Combine mashed potatoes with sauteed onions. Put in greased baking dish and brown in oven for 30 minutes at 350 degrees.

JACK KLUGMAN/Kasha Varnishka

The Solitary Eater

When my father died, my mother, who had six children to raise, turned the living room into a millinery store. She was a very good hat maker.

The six of us never came home at the same time so she would feed us as we came in. Because she couldn't make mashed potatoes for each of us individually, she would make a whole batch of mashed potatoes. When one of us came in, she would put down the thimble, come into the kitchen and dish out the food. Whoever came home first would have fresh, warm potatoes, but by the time the last one wandered in, the food was dry and cold. It was like going to a cafeteria.

When my rich uncle came over (at Chanuka he would give us $50), we would all sit around the table together. But aside from that, unless I went to a restaurant with my brother, I always ate alone.

Kasha Varnishka   • Serves 8

This may be prepared in the morning and heated when ready to serve.

1½ cups kasha (medium)
2 medium onions, chopped
2 tablespoons oil
1 4-ounce can mushrooms (stems and pieces), drained
1 4-ounce can whole mushrooms, drained
2 cups small shells, cooked and drained
1 tablespoons schmaltz (chicken fat)
Salt and pepper to taste

Method: Cook kasha according to instructions on box. Saute chopped onions in 2 tablespoons oil until golden brown. Add drained mushrooms. Cook 5 minutes longer. Mix kasha, shells, sauteed onions, chicken fat, salt and pepper.

The drained liquid from the canned mushrooms may be used as part of liquid in which kasha is cooked.

MICHELE LEE/Stuffed Tomatoes

The Kosher Nostra

All my life I have been a pasta freak. Even before I married James Farrentino, who made it official. Though I was brought up in Los Angeles, my mother and aunt had lived in the Bronx. Their next-door neighbor, who was Italian, made fantastically aromatic dishes, and the smell of her cooking filled the halls of the building. In the Bronx, it's possible to live next door to someone for years and never meet them. So one day, my mother and aunt camped outside the neighbor's door and when she came out, they confronted her. Before they could explain why they were there, the neighbor asked if she could get some recipes for Jewish cooking—"You know," she said, "the smell in our halls is just fantastic."

This lady had a great influence on their cooking, and many Italian-kosher recipes were created by this Roman-Jewish liaison. This recipe is from Venice, where the neighbor came from, and it's one I've transported to the West Coast.

Stuffed Tomatoes • Serves 4

2 cups tomato juice
1/8 teaspoon cinnamon
   **Few grains garlic powder (or ½ clove fresh
   garlic, put through press)**
¾ teaspoon salt
½ teaspoon pepper
4 tablespoons olive oil
1 cup converted or long grain rice
4 large tomatoes, or 6 to 8 small tomatoes
1 tablespoon chopped parsley

Method: Bring tomato juice, cinnamon, garlic powder or garlic, and salt and pepper to a rapid boil in a pot with a close-fitting lid. Add 2 tablespoons of the olive oil. Add rice to boiling tomato juice. Level rice with a fork so that it covers bottom of pot evenly. Reduce heat to simmer. Cover pot and cook rice till tender and all juice is absorbed (about 25 minutes). (Don't lift cover during cooking). Cut off tops of tomatoes and reserve. Scoop out pulp, and discard seeds. Cut tomato pulp into small pieces. Combine pulp with cooked rice. Add parsley. Stuff tomatoes with rice mixture. Sprinkle with remaining 2 tablespoons olive oil. Cover tomatoes with their tops. Place in well-oiled baking dish. Bake in 400-degree oven 10 to 12 minutes until hot.

WALTER MATTHAU/Kasha (Groats)

Mother Matthau's Meat Loaf

My mother didn't know how to cook anything. She never used the oven, only the top of the stove. An example of her great dishes was steamed meat loaf. She mushed everything together, made sort of a cake, put it in with whole carrots, little potatoes and whole onions, and steamed it.

When my daughter, Jennie, was about nine, I brought her to grandma's. She was wearing blue jeans. We were served momma's favorite— steamed meat loaf and the steamed vegetables. After the meal, I noticed a large wet spot on Jennie's back pocket. "What have you got in there, Jennie?" I asked.

She said, "Shh, don't tell grandma. Please, don't tell grandma."

When we got outside, I discovered she had put the meat loaf, turnips, carrots, peas and everything in her pocket. What do kids know about gourmet cooking?

Kasha (Groats)   • Serves 4-6

1 cup whole groats
2 eggs
2 cups boiling chicken broth
   Salt to taste

Method: Put groats into large colander and run water through them as rapidly as possible to wash off starch. Drain well. Combine eggs with groats. Put groat mixture into very hot saucepan. Separate with fork. Toss and cook until groats are separate, dry and firm. Pour boiling chicken broth into groats. Season with salt. Turn heat down to simmer and cook, covered, 15 to 20 minutes.

NEHEMIAH PERSOFF/Mushrooms and Potatoes

The Jerusalem Connection

My grandmother's chief occupation around the house in Jerusalem was peeling potatoes. Mushrooms and potatoes were eaten almost every night following the rains after Rosh Hashanah. My mother must have been pleased because potatoes were cheap and mushrooms which used to grow in the fields and in between the weeds were plentiful and free under every pine tree.

Grandmother would sit peeling potatoes at the gate of our house, where she also gossiped with her friends. She would talk to everyone who passed by and there was nobody she talked to who she didn't find out was a relative. She would find out that they came from Minsk or Pinsk, around the corner from Yankela's shoe store. Behind Yankela's shoe store, there was a little harness shop. It was run by Hymie the Hinkadinka, and maybe he was uncle of my granduncle. And behind Hymie the Hinkadinka's harness shop, there was Tuva the Toiba's tailor shop, and perhaps he was a cousin to a Tante Tessie's brother-in-law Shmeryl. And it is entirely possible that Shmeryl was Rivka's third husband. And Rivka was Rochl's grandaunt, twice removed. And who was Rochl, you might ask? I'll tell you. I don't know. But she must have been a relative, because grandmother said so.

Mushrooms and Potatoes

• Serves 8-10

12 medium potatoes
   Lightly salted water to cover potatoes
3 tablespoons chicken fat
2 tablespoons margarine
2 cups finely diced onions
½ pound mushrooms, sliced (the more you picked
   up, the more you used)
   Salt and pepper to taste
2 tablespoons chopped parsley

Method: Peel potatoes and cut into approximately 1-inch pieces. Boil in lightly salted water. When almost tender, drain. In mixture of fat and margarine, saute onions until golden brown. Add sliced mushrooms; saute about 5 minutes. Add salt and pepper to taste and approximately 2 tablespoons water. Let simmer about 2 minutes. Pour other vegetables on top of potatoes. Toss gently. Using very low flame, cook until potatoes are completely done. Place on serving dish and sprinkle with parsley before serving.

DON RICKLES/Kasha

The Jewish Den Mother

My mother, Etta Rickles, traveled with me for the first fifteen years of my career—that is, BB (Before Barbara). Wherever I played, she cooked for me. When word got out that I was to appear in a certain city, my phone started ringing with dinner reservations from other acts booked into that area.

Among my mother's proudest possessions are my friends' thank-you notes for her dinners. She has a photo from Jackie Cooper which says: "With much love for the friendship . . . and the pot roast." There is one from Sinatra. When he was sick he called us at 2 a.m. Etta got the word and prepared some chicken soup, carrots and all, and sent it over. The note she received the following day read: "Truly enjoyed the soup . . . but I feel I must tell you—my friends had more than their share!" Lucille Ball and Gary Morton sent her a thank-you for her chopped liver. After eating her kasha you'll want to send her one, too.

Kasha   • Serves 6-8

1 egg
1 cup medium buckwheat groats
2 cups boiling water
5 onions, cut up and sauteed in 2 to 3 tablespoons oil till golden
½ pound box of bows, cooked and drained
Salt and pepper to taste

Method: On very low flame, mix 1 raw egg into 1 cup of groats, stirring all the time until groats are dry. Add two cups boiling water to groats and stir once. Cover pot and let cook on low heat 15 minutes. Turn off heat. Add sauteed onions and cooked, drained bows. Toss to combine. Season to taste with salt and pepper.

This can be made in advance and reheated in a casserole in a 325-degree oven.

MRS. RICHARD TUCKER/Noodle Pudding

Landsman

My husband, Richard, was a Roumanian, and like all people from that country loved good food and wine. The Roumanians are happy and convivial people who savor every moment of life.

When we made our first trip to Israel, the stewardess said, "Shalom." And before we even took off, we were filled with emotion. As soon as Richard set foot on Israeli soil, he knew he was home.

It was a pleasure to eat in Israel. The people are so happy to serve you. After one particularly delicious meal, we engaged in conversation with the owner, and to our delight found out he was from —where else?—Roumania.

Noodle Pudding • Serves 8-10

1 pound medium egg noodles
1 cup crushed pineapple
1 16-ounce can mixed fruit cocktail (drained)
1 apple, peeled and sliced thin
½ cup maraschino cherries (cut small) and juice
3 eggs, separated
¾ cup sugar
1½ teaspoons vanilla
    Dash of cinnamon
1 teaspoon salt

Method: Boil noodles in salt water till soft. Drain and add all fruit, egg yolks and spices to noodles. Beat whites till stiff and fold into mixture. Pour into greased 8 x 12-inch baking dish. Bake in pre-heated 350-degree oven 50 minutes or until golden brown. Cut into squares.

BLINTZES, PANCAKES, MATZOS

MARTY ALLEN • Spinach "Surprise" Pancakes
MOREY AMSTERDAM • Matzo Schalet
SAMMY CAHN • Matzo Brie
MARILYN HALL • Challa
SENATOR JACOB K. JAVITS • Cheese Blintzes
HAL LINDEN • Cheese-Mustard Loaf
ROSS MARTIN • Fleishidike Matzos
          (Non-dairy Matzos)
JEAN NIDETCH • Cheese Latkes (Pancakes)
IRVING WALLACE • Wonderful Matzo Brie

MARTY ALLEN/Spinach "Surprise" Pancakes

A Habit I Never Should Have Broken

When I was in high school, I used to give away my sandwiches to the poor kids who couldn't afford to bring a full lunch to school. My mother always wondered why I was so skinny.

Today, most of my high school buddies are married, doing well and can afford to buy their own lunches. Frenchie prepares my food now and, as anyone can see, I am making up for all those lunches I gave away.

Spinach "Surprise" Pancakes • Serves 4

⅓ head lettuce
½ medium onion
2 medium potatoes
3 carrots
2 cups fresh spinach
2 eggs, well beaten
1 cup all-purpose flour
½ teaspoon salt
   Sprinkle pepper, if desired
   Sour cream
4 tablespoons margarine or butter
4 tablespoons oil

Method: With fine blade of grinder, grind together lettuce, onion, potatoes, carrots and spinach. Add well-beaten eggs. Sift together flour and salt and fold into vegetable mixture. Add pepper if used. Drop by spoonfuls into heated, greased pan and cook until golden brown. Serve with sour cream.

MOREY AMSTERDAM/Matzo Schalet

Can You Top This?

I was born in Chicago, but at the age of two I was smart enough to pack the family up and move to San Francisco.

For 35 years, my father was concertmaster of the San Francisco Symphony Orchestra. Because we always had company—we had guests in our house like Caruso, Lily Pons, Paderewski—one of my most vivid memories is the smell of perking coffee. My mother always rose to the occasion because she was an international cook who would happily make delicacies like calf brains and eggs for my father's breakfast. One day I overheard my mother placing an order with the butcher on the telephone.

"Hello, have you got any brains . . .?"

She stopped and quickly corrected herself:

"I mean, have you got any brains *at all?*"

I fell off the couch laughing, and she was too embarrassed to face the butcher for weeks.

Matzo Schalet   Serves 6-8

2 matzos
2 tablespoons vegetable shortening
2 tablespoons sugar
¼ teaspoon salt
2 tablespoons raisins
2 tablespoons dried currants
2 tablespoons ground almonds
¼ teaspoon cinnamon
1 large apple, diced
3 eggs, separated

Method: Soak broken matzos in cold water and when soft, squeeze dry. Add vegetable shortening, sugar, salt, raisins, currants, ground almonds and cinnamon. Add the diced apple and beaten egg yolks and finally fold in the stiffly beaten whites. Bake in greased 6-inch pudding dish in moderate oven (350 degrees) for 45 minutes.

SAMMY CAHN/Matzo Brie

The Miracle in Sheepshead Bay, or A Story with a Twist

I remember vividly, having bought my mother Elka and father Ave (a lovely gentle man) and my four sisters, Sadye, Pearl, Florence and Evelyn, their first home in Sheepshead Bay, Brooklyn, N.Y. I also remember their shrieks of joy over the house, which had two stories and a "finished basement" with its very own little kitchen.

The kitchen, as you can imagine, had a tiny stove—just two burners and an oven. I would guess its total dimensions were two feet long by about a foot and a half deep. Into this oven every Friday afternoon, Elka would place her special braided challa—a traditional must for the Friday evening dinner along with the gefilte fish and lukshen soup and boiled chicken. Every Friday at about mid-afternoon Elka ever so gently placed the baking pan with the braided challa into this two and a half foot oven. That evening she would bring the miracle to the table—a three-foot long challa! I have tried for years to figure that out.

Matzo Brie
• Serves 3-4

4-5 sheets of matzo
  Warm water
  Eggs (one less than number of sheets of matzo)
  Salt and pepper to taste
  Butter
  Sour cream, jam, brown sugar or applesauce

Method: Break large pieces of matzo into mixing bowl. Pour water over matzo and soak until soft; pour into cloth and squeeze out water. Beat eggs in mixing bowl; add salt and pepper to taste. Then put matzo into eggs and mix. Warm frying pan, put in ¼ pound of butter and melt. (Chicken fat can be used instead of butter.) Add matzo-egg mixture, cover and cook over very low flame, turning frequently and adding butter to facilitate turning. Serve with sour cream or jam, brown sugar or applesauce.

MARILYN HALL/Challa

Looking Back

Memories of 146 Eastbourne Avenue in Toronto on those crackling winter nights, walking on snow that squeaked, noses pinched, foggy puffs of breath that lead you home to hot chocolate, crackers and butter. Washing dishes in a sudsy pot in the porcelain sink, the rinse pan next, then the rack on the drainboard—wash, rinse, rack—wash, rinse, rack—a litany not unlike a montra of today that lulls you into calming dreams and thoughts of summer. Summer—and plump loganberry and raspberry bushes behind the garage, giving up fruit that tastes of sunshine. The most silent sound in the world—one berry falling on another in the breakfast cereal bowl.

Mother and her pressure cooker—the precarious whistle that rushed one to the stove before the lid blew off. Mother and her waterless cooker and sedimented vegetables—the nutrition going down the drain. The drain never had a virus. It was the healthiest thing in the house. My sister and I survived gallons of cod liver oil that supposedly got us through the winter. Mother and her bird-like portions and the ritualistic excuse of Monty, my husband-to-be, after an invited meal—a mumbled pardon about having to mail a letter when he actually went to a local hamburger restaurant to whomp down enough food to carry him through the evening.

The breakfast nook—a table and wooden seats that lifted up to reveal a catch-all of magazines, party favors, seed catalogs and half-eaten arrowroot cookies, gumdrops, hair nets, string, shuttlecocks, volleyballs, skate guards. The Board of Health would have condemned it. The dining room was like a poor relative who hung around waiting to be asked to the party in the kitchen. It was all dressed up with gleaming silver and English china, but had no place to go. I remember the summer kitchen and the icebox with the fan on top and the tap that groaned when you turned the water on. I remember those times and wonder if the present owners hear the echoes.

Challa

½ cup oil
4 teaspoons salt
1 tablespoon sugar
1 cup boiling water
½ cup cold water
2 packages dry yeast
⅓ cup warm water
3 eggs
7 cups flour (unbleached)
  Sesame or poppy seeds

Method: Pour the oil, salt and sugar into a large mixing bowl. Add 1 cup boiling water and stir; add ½ cup cold water. Dissolve 2 packages dry yeast in ⅓ cup warm water. Beat 3 eggs and add to oil and water mixture, saving 1 tablespoon of beaten egg to be brushed on loaves before baking. Add dissolved yeast and stir. Add 7 cups of unbleached flour and mix well. Turn out on floured board and knead until dough does not stick to board or hands. Add more flour if necessary. Return dough to bowl and cover with a clean towel. Place in oven that has been preheated for 1 minute and then turned off. Let dough rise for 1 hour. It will double in bulk. If poked with finger, the hole will remain. Turn dough out on lightly floured board and knead for about 1 minute. Cut into 12 equal pieces and knead each piece with a little flour until it is not sticky. Let rest while you grease a cookie sheet with vegetable shortening. Roll each piece of dough into a strand about 8 inches long. Make four braided loaves. Place on baking sheet and let rise for 45 minutes at room temperature. Brush tops of loaves with beaten egg and sprinkle with sesame or poppy seeds. Bake in 375-degree oven for 40 minutes. Remove loaves to racks to cool.

Extra loaves may be stored in freezer. Frozen loaves should be thawed and placed in oven for 5 to 10 minutes.

SENATOR JACOB K. JAVITS/Cheese Blintzes

A Capitol Recipe

The following recipe was contributed by Senator Javits, with a note that it was a favorite recipe that he enjoyed in his youth. He did not indicate whether it is currently on the menu in the Senatorial dining room.

Cheese Blintzes
Filling

1 pound dry cottage cheese
2 egg yolks, well beaten
1 tablespoon butter, melted
1 tablespoon sugar (more if preferred)
  Salt to taste

Batter

1¼ cup milk (can use skim)
1 teaspoons slat
2 whole eggs plus 2 whites, well beaten
1 cup flour
  Butter or shortening

Other Ingredients
  Sour cream
  Frozen strawberries

Method: Cream cottage cheese with fork until very smooth. Add egg yolks, melted butter and sugar and salt to taste. Make batter by adding milk to salt, eggs and egg whites. Stir flour in gradually until mixture is smooth. Allow batter to rest for an hour. Heat 10-inch frying pan; grease lightly with shortening or butter. Pour enough batter to make a very thin pancake (similar to a crepe), tipping pan quickly to cover bottom completely. Cook until underside is lightly browned. Flip out onto dry surface, browned side up. Place a heaping tablespoon of the filling in center of each pancake; fold from both sides, then into envelope shape. Proceed in this way until all batter has been used. Just before serving, fry blintzes on both sides in butter (or arrange blintzes in a shallow casserole, dot with butter and bake in 400-degree oven) until golden brown. Serve hot with sour cream and defrosted frozen strawberries.

Makes approximately 7 to 9 large blintzes.

HAL LINDEN/Cheese-Mustard Loaf

The Patchwork Seder

Years ago, when the week's activity consisted of four days of making rounds and one day at the unemployment office, several friends and I would get our families together for communal holiday celebrations.

When Passover came around, we had an invitational seder. The responsibility of preparing the main dish was ours, but it was the other dishes that provided the excitement. Mrs. Joe Raposo was to bring the chicken soup. I mean, zuppa alla cacciatore chicken soup is a bit extreme for the ordinary seder table; and her arangi matzo balls— incredible! And Mrs. Dick O'Neill's charosis—every year the same delicious charosis. It was so good that no one ever asked her how come it was green.

This recipe was our contribution at Christmas tree trimming time. I especially recommend it for unemployed actors.

Cheese-Mustard Loaf

1 loaf unsliced bakery bread (day-old cuts best)
½ pound (8 slices) jack cheese
½ pound (8 slices) American cheese
1 cup softened butter or margarine
⅔ cup finely minced onions
6 tablespoons prepared mustard
2 tablespoons poppy seeds
4 teaspoons lemon juice
½ teaspoon monosodium glutamate (optional)

Method: Make eight diagonal equal cuts in bread almost to bottom. Mix butter, onions, mustard, poppy seeds and lemon juice. Spread a few table-spoons of mixture into slices. Reserve the rest. Sprinkle cheese slices with monosodium gluta-mate. Place one slice of each cheese in each cut. Press bread together (Tie with string for firm hold.) Place in shallow greased baking pan or on cookie sheet. Spread rest of butter mixture on top and sides of bread. Bake in 350-degree oven 20 minutes or until slightly brown and cheese has melted. Serve with salad. Makes 9 slices.

ROSS MARTIN/Fleishidike Matzos

The Formula

The first three years of my life, my parents and I lived with my grandmother in a flat on New York's lower East Side. The cooking, done over a coal-burning black stove, was a kind of joint venture shared by my mother and grandmother.

This side-by-side learning resulted in a purely kinesthetic cooking—where things are done by feel, not measure. My mother's recipes, therefore, have instructions like "you'll shake in a little," and should you ask her how much is a little, her only answer would be, "You'll see—how much you need."

On those rare occasions when one of her dishes turned out below her standard of perfection, her disappointment was couched gently in one rueful sentence: "It isn't faithful to me this time."

Herewith, one of her simpler dishes, the mere memory of which even now reaches over the years and pulls me instantly back to my childhood in that warm little room beside that big black stove.

Fleishidike Matzos (Non-dairy Matzos)

• Serves 4

4 eggs
Salt and pepper to taste
Matzo meal (about 2 tablespoons)
1 medium large onion, grated
4 whole matzos, dampened with water to soften slightly
½ teaspoon chicken fat
3 tablespoons oil

Method: Beat eggs well and add salt and pepper to taste. Add enough matzo meal to thicken mixture a little; it will still be fairly runny. Grate onion and add to mixture, mixing thoroughly. Baste each whole dampened matzo thoroughly with the egg mixture, making sure all are well covered. Heat chicken fat (if used) and oil over a high flame in a large frying pan. Put in sheet of matzo; fry until brown. Turn over and fry other side until brown. Serve immediately.

JEAN NIDETCH/Cheese Latkes

Overseas but Underweight

I recently returned from a six-country tour of Europe. Every time I ate in a fancy French restaurant, it was a challenge to eat safely and not fattening. I ate broiled fish and veal in every country, so my impression of European food is all the same. Dieters too are the same throughout the world. They all raid their refrigerators in the middle of the night.

Cheese Latkes (Pancakes)   • Serves 1

1 egg, well beaten
⅓ cup cottage cheese
⅓ cup skim milk
¼ teaspoon salt
1 slice bread, made into crumbs
    Blueberry topping (recipe below)

Method: Combine all ingredients except topping and mix well. Drop by spoonfuls onto hot nonstick pan. Brown lightly on both sides. Serve with blueberry topping.

Blueberry Topping

½ cup blueberries
1 tablespoon water
    Artificial sweetener to equal 2 teaspoons sugar

Method: Combine ingredients in saucepan, cover and simmer slowly until berries are soft.

IRVING WALLACE/Wonderful Matzo Brie

I Remember Mama

Memories of my mother, Bessie Wallace—she died five years ago—often relate her to the background of a spic-and-span kitchen, one of the few places where she had complete self-assurance. She was a wonderful cook, especially of dishes that she herself enjoyed. Her specialty was a fantastic strudel large enough to serve a dozen people. The strudel brings to mind one particular memory.

We were in our bungalow in Kenosha, Wisconsin, and it was afternoon, and my mother had spread out on the wooden kitchen table the dough for a strudel that covered the entire surface. I, perhaps a boy of twelve, perched on a stool nearby, watching with awe, as she began to sprinkle the dough with the nuts, fruits, assorted goodies that would compose the anatomy of a perfect strudel.

It was an afternoon when she had many in-coming phone calls. During the first phone call, she became deeply engaged in conversation, and as she held the phone in her left hand, talking, she absently reached out with her right hand to steadily munch away at the fillings atop the strudel dough. There were four more successive phone calls, and during each she talked and nibbled. At last the calls came to an end, and she turned to concentrate on her strudel. "Now we're going to roll it up and bake it," she said to me. She bent to start rolling it—then stood stunned. There was no filling left. None whatsoever. Only the naked dough.

That night we had a strudelless dinner. We had matzo brie for our main course—*and* for desert

As I said, my mother loved to cook what she enjoyed eating. And that was one time she enjoyed too much.

Wonderful Matzo Brie

4 whole matzos
1 cup milk
8 eggs, well beaten
½ teaspoon pepper
½ teaspoon salt
1 teaspoon garlic salt
2 tablespoons margarine or butter

• Serves 4-6

Method: Break matzos into pieces roughly an inch in size. Heat milk and soak matzo pieces in warm milk about 5 minutes. Drop soaked matzos into a pan and pour beaten eggs over them. Add pepper, salt and garlic salt. Melt butter and add to mixture of matzos and eggs. Cook at low heat, stirring occasionally until eggs are set. Serve and eat while hot.

DESSERTS AND BEVERAGES

MARILYN BERGMAN • Lyrical Lime Pie
LLOYD BOCHNER • Persimmon Pudding
JACK CARTER • Fresh Fruit Kuchen
LEE J. COBB • Strudel
RABBI JEROME CUTLER • Gogl-Mogl
BETTY GARRETT • Home Brew
VIRGINIA GRAHAM • Coffee Toffee Pie
MARILYN HALL • Cold Schav (Sorrel)
FLORENCE HENDERSON • Blueberry Souffle
MADELINE KAHN • Foot Cookies
JERRY LEWIS • Vinegar Chocolate Cake
WALTER MATTHAU • Raspberry Tea
RHODA MORGENSTERN • Kahlua Ice Cream
Special
TONY RANDALL • Cherry Cheese Graham Cracker
Pie
DINAH SHORE • Pecan Rum Cakes
ELKE SOMMER • German Coffee Cake
MARK SPITZ • Carrot Ring
MEL TORME • Yellow Cake with Chocolate Icing
ELI WALLACH • Non-dairy Date and Nut Bread
GENE WILDER • Mock Strudel

MARILYN BERGMAN/Lyrical Lime Pie

The Way It Was

Didn't everyone's grandma live with them after Grandpa died? Wasn't everyone's kitchen like a battleground with *her* side and your mother's side? The drawers with *her* flatware, the cupboard with *her* pots and pans and dishes, *her* dishtowels? *Her* side of the sink with the red-marked soap and the blue-marked soap? All as far away from ours as the tight quarters would allow? (Even though, out of love for her, we would never have pork or shellfish or any of those forbiddens—Oh, the heaven of a bacon, lettuce and tomato down at the corner drugstore or at a friend's house!)

Didn't everyone think that all meat had to be placed on a board (slanted by putting a plate on the side farthest from the sink), salted and left to sit until all the blood ran out and then wrung dry? That vegetables started their long boil at four o'clock to be ready for dinner at six? (Green beans may have started out green but were never eaten that way! Did you eat meat red?) Didn't everyone's garden have at least one fork or spoon planted along with the hollyhocks because *you* had

accidentally mixed one of *hers* with one of *yours*, and it had to be restored to its state of purity by 24 hours in the soil?

Didn't everyone?

Lyrical Lime Pie

1 box (8-ounce) chocolate wafers
½ cup unsalted butter or margarine, melted
    Filling (recipe below)

Method: Place wafers in strong plastic bag and crush finely with rolling pin, or use food mill. Add melted butter or margarine and blend well. Press mixture firmly to sides and bottom of 10-inch pie plate. Bake at 350 degrees 10 minutes. Cool before filling.

Filling

1 (14-ounce) can condensed milk
⅓ cup fresh lime juice (about 3 limes)
1 tablespoon grated lime rind

3 eggs, separated
3-4 drops green food coloring
¼ teaspoon salt
1 cup whipping cream, whipped and flavored
with 2 tablespoons powdered sugar and ½
teaspoon vanilla
Grated semi-sweet chocolate

Method: Mix condensed milk with lime juice, 1½ teaspoons lime rind, and beaten egg yolks. Add coloring and mix well. Beat egg whites and salt until stiff (but not dry) and fold in. Pour into cool shell and bake 10 minutes at 250 degrees. Chill and top with whipped cream. Sprinkle with grated chocolate and remaining lime rind.

LLOYD BOCHNER/Persimmon Pudding

My Grandmother's Kitchen

Of all the things that I recall
From years ago when I was small,
One that stands out from all the others
Is the marvelous kitchen at my grandmother's.

A place of love, of warmth, of caring
Of knishes, farfel, of pickled herring,
Of matzo balls, both light and soggy,
And a strange dish they called fisnogy.

Of pirogen, kichels, cherry strudel,
Of chicken soup both plain and noodle,
Of borscht, two kinds—white and red,
Of horseradish that would clear your head.

Of kugels, latkes and cheese blintzes
(Would please the palate of a Jewish princess),
Of gefilte fish, gehacte leber,
(Better made than Golde's, her next door neighbor).

Of festive meals, aunts, uncles, cousins,
It seemed at times that there were dozens
All gathered round the linened table
To eat much more than they were able.

But all that's passed. Gone is the joy
Of Bubby's kitchen when I was a boy.
Her spirit lives on, for at times, I confess,
I catch myself saying, "Mein kindt, ess ess!"

Persimmon Pudding

1½ cup flour, sifted
1¼ cup sugar
1 teaspoon baking soda
½ teaspoon salt
2 teaspoons cinnamon
1 teaspoon ginger
½ teaspoon nutmeg
½ cup melted butter
2½ cups rich milk
3 eggs, beaten
1 quart persimmons (very ripe), sieved
1 cup raisins and/or chopped nuts (optional)

Method: Combine and sift together flour, sugar, baking powder, soda, salt, cinnamon, ginger and nutmeg. Combine melted butter, milk, eggs and persimmons. Fold liquid mixture into dry ingredients. Combine completely. Fold in raisins and nuts, if used. Bake in 325-degree oven 1½ hours or until a cake tester comes out clean when cake is tested.

JACK CARTER/Fresh Fruit Kuchen

My Mother the Ump

I love noodle pudding—especially my wife's. That is, when I get to taste it, for when Roxanne makes it she runs all over the neighborhood to give everyone a sample. When she comes home, I get to lick the dish.

My mother serves "Watch-Out Food." We don't get courses in our house; we get threats: Watch out for the chicken—there's bones. Watch out for the soup—it's too hot. Don't eat the dessert—you'll fill yourself up. Nem nisht broit (don't take bread). The potatoes are coming. So I always leave there starving. I have to go to a restaurant to eat. Then she says, "See. You didn't eat too much. You won't get sick." Then she serves the same meal to the next person. She stands behind me—"The bones—you'll choke!" "Mom, I'm 47. I know a bone." I don't have a mother; I have an umpire.

Once I took Rex Harrison to Lindy's for a Jewish meal. He looked at the menu, "I think I'd like some fish." I said, "Let me order for you." "No thanks," he said. "I've ordered fish throughout the world. Waiter, I'd like an order of 'geflute!'"

Fresh Fruit Kuchen   • Serves 6-8

1 cup flour
1 stick butter (½ cup)
¼ cup sugar
2 cups fresh peaches, plums, apricots, or any fresh fruit of your choice, sliced
2 beaten eggs
½ cup sugar, or to taste depending on sweetness of fruit
1 teaspoon vanilla
Drop of almond flavoring (go lightly or it will take over)

Method: Combine flour, butter and ¼ cup sugar with your fingers till mixture is crumbly. Press into a 12 x 12-inch pan. Bake in 350-degree oven till dough is tinged with gold. While this is baking, combine beaten eggs, sugar, vanilla and drop of almond flavoring. Add fruit mixture. Pour onto gold-tinged crust. Put back into oven and bake till fruit mixture and eggs are set—about 30 minutes. Cool before cutting into squares.

LEE COBB/Strudel

Better Than Anyone

My mother originally came from Russia, but due to the trauma of a Jewish family constantly wandering, as a child she was abandoned in Constantinople.

Eventually she made her way to New York, married my father, who was from Russian Roumania, and they settled on the East Side. Mother was too busy making things work for the family to learn to read and write, and as a child I taught her to speak English. It was a rough neighborhood, and you had to be resourceful to survive. She was certainly experienced at that and her practicality held the family together.

I suppose like most mothers, my mother made some things better than anyone else in the world. Her strudel was not simply an apple cake; hers was a real production. She used many nuts and raisins, and the finished product was always "bitier."

Strudel
• Serves 10

½ cup lukewarm water
1 tablespoon vegetable oil or melted butter
1 egg
¼ teaspoon salt
2 cups flour
About 1 cup oil or melted butter
Strudel filling (recipes follow)

Method: Mix together water, 1 tablespoon oil or melted butter and egg and salt. Sift flour onto a board, letting it pile up into a mound. Make a well in the center of the mound and slowly pour the liquid into the well. Mix quickly with a knife, then knead until dough is smooth and elastic and does not stick to board. Flour another board well and toss dough onto it. Cover dough with a hot bowl and let rest in a warm place 30 minutes. Prepare filling for strudel while dough is resting. (See recipes for fillings.) Roll dough out and stretch it, working quickly. This is done as follows: cover a table with a cloth, flour the cloth well, place dough in center and roll it out with a rolling pin as thin as possible without breaking it. Brush surface of rolled-out dough lightly with oil or melted butter (about ¼ cup). Place your hands, palms down, under dough and gently pull and stretch it toward yourself, being careful not to tear it. Shift your position and repeat procedure. Keep repeating it until you have gone completely around the table. By this time dough should be as think as a sheet of paper, except the edges, which will be thicker. Trim off edges. Trimming will be easier if the table you are working on is a little smaller than sheet of dough so that edges of sheet overlap table. Brush surface of sheet lightly with oil or melted butter again (about ¼ cup). Sprinkle sheet evenly with a strudel filling, leaving about one-quarter of the sheet unspread. Sprinkle filling with oil or melted butter (about ¼ cup). Fold the unspread one-quarter of the sheet forward over filling. Lift tablecloth with both hands, and when you have lifted it high enough, strudel will begin to roll over upon itself. Keep lifting tablecloth, and strudel will roll over and over until it forms a large roll. Trim off ends of roll and cut it two or three times to fit baking pan. Pan should be a shallow one and greased (a cookie sheet is fine). Place pan at edge of table and roll strudel into it. Work quickly all the time. Brush top of strudel with oil or melted butter. Bake at 375 degrees 45 minutes or until brown and crisp, basting occasionally with oil or melted butter.

Filling I (Apple)

7 cups apples, chopped fine
1 cup seedless raisins, cut
½ cup currants
1 cup sugar
1 teaspoon cinnamon
½ cup ground nuts

Combine all ingredients.

Filling II (Cheese)

2 pounds cottage cheese, drained, or use farmer cheese
Yolks of 4 eggs
Whites of 2 eggs
2 tablespoons sour cream
Salt and sugar to taste
Grated rind of ½ lemon, if desired
Sugar, seedless raisins, ground almonds

Method: Pass cheese through a sieve and mix with remaining ingredients in order named. If richer and sweeter strudel is desired, add more sugar, ½ cup seedless raisins and 1 cup ground almonds.

RABBI JEROME CUTLER/Gogl-Mogl

Playing the Catskills

Jackie, Velvel, Barry, LeRoy, Hilton Milton, Milty Hilty, the Parness Boys and me. We made up the elite waiter and busboy staff at the Pioneer Country Club in the renowned Catskills. Jackie Miller, who was studying to be a surgeon, worked as a waiter, and I was his busboy. Whenever Jackie wasn't around, I would tell the people sitting at our tables that Jackie was going to be a great surgeon someday, and God forbid if they needed a surgeon in a few years and it turned out to be Jackie, he would remember if they tipped good or bad.

We always did well!

And how many times did I hear a woman turn to her husband as they were checking out and ask in Yiddish, "Mendl, did you leave the busboy?"

"What then," would come the irritated reply, "we should take him with us?"

Gogl-Mogl

1 egg
½ cup milk
½ cup ice cream
1 ripe peach, blanched and cut
   Honey and sugar to taste

Method: Combine all ingredients in blender.

Old-Time Gogl-Mogl

1 or 2 eggs
1 cup milk
½ teaspoon vanilla
   Honey to taste

Method: Whip all ingredients with eggbeater till foamy. Serve hot.

BETTY GARRETT/Home Brew

Hopping Glad

When Larry Parks and I decided to make beer, we were innocents. I think we thought we were doing something illegal. In truth, you are allowed by law to make a certain amount of beer and wine for home consumption as long as you don't sell it. We proceeded as though we were performing a religious ritual. We followed every step of the enclosed recipe, put in our mash and brew tester (hydrometer) and waited for it to sink to the red line. When it got close, it happened to be our bedtime, and we were worried that the crucial moment would happen during the night and we would miss the perfect bottling time. So we set our alarm clock to ring every hour during the night and took turns gettng up.

I remember being awakened at 1 a.m. by a slight nudge and a whisper—"It's not ready yet." I did the same for Larry at 2 a.m. And so on until morning. It turned out that last centimeters until the hydrometer sinks to the red line takes hours! The brew was finally ready at 8:30 a.m.

The first batch gots its first tasting at two weeks. We couldn't wait the full three! It was delicious—though it does get better with age. And a warning: it is *much* stronger than store-bought beer—so watch it!

We made it with *less* malt for light beer, *more* malt for dark beer—and it was always the best beer I ever tasted. (One time we made it so light we passed if off as champagne and got away with it!)

All I can say is, the family that makes beer together has a heck of a lot of fun!

Home Brew

Requires several weeks preparation.
The only trouble with this recipe is you need to buy special equipment. But if you like beer, it's worth it. You need:

12-gallon or 6-gallon crock
  Large cooking pot, not aluminum (porcelain or granite caps
  Bottles; ½ pint, 1 pint or both

Bottle caps
Bottle capper
Hydrometer (or mash and brew taster, as it is
called in the recipe)
Length of rubber hose with clamp or clothes pin

(Never use cane or beet sugar in this recipe)
For 12-gallon crock

8 pounds corn sugar (Never use cane or beet sugar
    in this recipe)
1 bag seedless hops
1 can supreme malt
1 yeast cake
2 envelopes Knox Gelatin (optional)

Method: Dissolve supreme malt in boiling water.
Dissolve corn sugar in boiling water. Put the
dissolved malt and corn sugar in crock. Put hops in
cloth and tie with string to make a large tea bag. Put
this in hot water and simmer for 10 minutes. (Do not
boil hops.) Squeeze bag. Let drain out, throw bag
away and add the hops liquid to solution in crock.
Add enough cold water to solution to make it all
lukewarm. Fill crock 2 inches from top of crock.

Dissolve yeast cake in cup of lukewarm water and
add this to brew. Stir.

First morning, skim off froth from top of crock,
with spoon, after do not molest until ready to
bottle. Use mash and brew tester to tell when to
bottle for accuracy at the red line. If you wait too
long and tester sinks past red line too far, add ¼
teaspoon corn sugar to pint bottle or ½ teaspoon to
a quart bottle. This will keep brew from being flat.
Gelatin may be used to settle yeast, by thoroughly
dissolving 2 envelopes Knox Gelatin into a sauce
pan with about 1 pint of warm water, then pour over
top of brew in crock a day or two before bottling.

After bottling let stand at least three weeks before
using. After two, three, four months, brew will
become 100 percent better and stronger.

Do not use aluminum pots when you simmer
hops, because it takes on a metallic taste.

Recipe for a 6-gallon crock

4 pounds corn sugar
½ bag seedless hops
½ can supreme malt
½ yeast cake
1 Envelope Knox Gelatin (Optional)

VIRGINIA GRAHAM/Coffee Toffee Pie

Sweet Rudolph

My childhood consisted of sponge cake as a confection madness, and on Sunday, confectioners sugar to denote the Sabbath. These palatal restrictions made me an early sweet-aholic.

This coffee pie was a childhood fantasy, later replaced by Rudolph Valentino. Were those really the good old days?

Coffee Toffee Pie   • Serves 12-15

Requires overnight preparation.

Pastry Shell

1 10-ounce package pie crust mix
½ cup firmly packed brown sugar
1½ cups walnuts, finely chopped
2 squares unsweetened chocolate, grated
2 teaspoons vanilla

Method: Combine all ingredients. Add 2 tablespoons water and mix well with a fork. Turn into 11-inch well-greased pie plate. Press firmly against bottom and side of plate. Bake 15 minutes in 375-degree oven. Cool on rack.

Filling

1 cup soft butter or margarine
1½ cups sugar
2 squares unsweetened chocolate (melted over double boiler and cooled)
4 teaspoons instant coffee (not freeze-dried)
4 eggs

Method: In large bowl, using electric mixer on medium speed, beat butter until creamy. Gradually add sugar. Beat until light. Blend in chocolate and instant coffee. Add eggs one at a time, beating slightly after each one. Then beat mixture for five more minutes. Pour into the cool pie shell. Put in refrigerator, covered, overnight. Next day make topping.

Topping

3 cups heavy cream
3 tablespoons instant coffee
¾ cup confectioners sugar

Method: Combine ingredients. Put in refrigerator for 2 hours. Beat until stiff. Put on pie with spoon or fancy No. 6 tip decorating bag. Decorate with shaved chocolate. Refrigerate at least 3 hours after adding topping.

MARILYN HALL/Cold Schav (Sorrel)

Lack of Communication

My mother-in-law once gave a dinner party which consisted of a whole poached salmon as the main dish. When it was cooked, she carefully arranged the fish on a platter and garnished it with hard-boiled eggs and pimientos. She instructed the new foreign-speaking maid to "put a little parsley in the mouth" just before she served it in the dining room.

After the first course, the dining room door swung open. The company was aghast. The maid was carrying the fish platter, and in *her* mouth were cunningly tucked some sprigs of parsley.

Cold Schav (Sorrel) • Serves 6

2 bunches sorrel
   Dollop of sour cream
1 cucumber, chopped fine
   Lemon juice
2 tablespoons sugar
   Salt to taste

Method: Cover sorrel with water, cook until tender. Strain, leaving some bits of green in liquid. Reserve liquid. Add sour cream, chopped cucumber, lemon juice, sugar and salt. Put into blender. Serve in tall, chilled glasses.

FLORENCE HENDERSON/Blueberry Souffle

A Nickle a Pickle

The first time I ate kosher food was when I started going with my husband Ira Bernstein and we visited his parents' home in Brooklyn. His mother made a terrific dish called Noodle Charlotte.

Before that the only kosher food I ever had was Jewish pickles, which are my absolute downfall. I could eat them by the barrelful. When I was on Broadway in the chorus of *Wish You Were Here*, Phyllis Newman and I would stop at the Gaiety Delicatessen just up the street from the Imperial Theatre and order pastrami sandwiches. The pastrami didn't thrill me that much. It was the pickle that came with the sandwich that I wanted.

I once had a Jewish girl friend whose mother used to send her a special Passover cake from Michigan, with orange peel and nuts. Delicious! You know, if religion could proselytize by food, Judaism could get a lot of converts.

Blueberry Souffle ● Serves 6

1 cup blueberries
  Heavy cream
2 tablespoons butter
3 tablespoons flour
1 teaspoon grated lemon rind
2 teaspoons lemon juice
4 egg yolks
½ cup sugar
6 egg whites
  Crushed blueberries
  Ice cream or sweetened kirsch- or
  cognac-flavored whipped cream

Method: Crush berries and add enough heavy cream to make 1¼ cups. Melt butter; add flour. Cook a moment or two and then add berry-cream mixture. Cook until thick, stirring constantly. Remove from heat and add lemon rind and juice. Beat egg yolks with ¼ cup of the sugar and add them to the blueberry mixture. Beat whites and gradually add the remaining ¼ cup of sugar and beat until stiff. Blend in blueberry mixture and turn into a buttered and sugared 1-quart souffle dish. Bake at 350 degrees 25 to 30 minutes. Serve at once. Serve with additional crushed berries which you have mixed with ice cream or sweetened and flavored (kirsch or cognac) whipped cream. (Whipped cream should be very cold.)

MADELINE KAHN/Foot Cookies

The Dough Toe

This is the only cooking idea I have originated. I had this concept and finally got up enough courage to call a company and ask them to make a cookie cutter in the shape of a footprint. After the initial shock, they agreed to make one, and we decided it would be the size of a small child's foot.

You don't need a foot cookie cutter to get foot cookies. After mixing up the cookie batter, just cut it into the shape of feet, bend the big toe in a little, scrunch up the little toe and make the second toe a little larger. Don't worry, slight flaws will enhance the design. Put a little pink food coloring on the ball and heel of the foot and then bake.

It's fun for me to watch people eat the Foot Cookies and to see which part they bite off first. The big toe is the most popular. When I brought my batch of cookies to the Dick Cavett Show New Year's Eve, they were described as "footies."

I could never bring myself to bite off the head of a gingerbread man but I decided I wouldn't mind eating a foot.

Foot Cookies

½ cup butter
1 cup sugar
1 tablespoon milk
2 beaten eggs
1 teaspoon vanilla
2½ cups flour
3 tablespoons baking powder

Method: Cream butter and add sugar, milk, beaten eggs and vanilla. Add flour and baking powder, mixed and sifted together. Roll out on floured board and cut with "foot" cookie cutter or your own foot design. Bake in 350-degree oven 10 minutes.

Makes 2 dozen, depending on size of cookies.

JERRY LEWIS/Vinegar Chocolate Cake

Mamma Was the Straight Man
by Mrs. Danny Lewis, Jerry's Mother

Every school day when my son came home, I would have a plate of sandwiches made for him with a large black and green olive on each one. He always took the olives and put them on the side of his plate. I asked him one day, "Why don't you eat the sandwiches with the olives?"

He replied, "I like the olives better than the sandwiches so I'm saving them for my dessert."

Vinegar Chocolate Cake • Serves 6

½ cup butter
1½ cups sugar
2 eggs
1 teaspoon vanilla

2 squares bitter chocolate melted in top of double boiler and cooled
2 cups sifted flour
½ teaspoon salt
1 cup sour milk
1 teaspoon baking soda
1 tablespoon vinegar

Method: Cream together butter and sugar until light and fluffy. Stir in eggs and vanilla and blend well. Add melted chocolate. Sift flour with salt and add to creamed mixture, alternately with sour milk. Mix together soda and vinegar and add to mixture. Pour into two greased 9-inch layer pans. Bake at 375 degrees 25 minutes or until a cake tester comes out clean.

WALTER MATTHAU/Raspberry Tea

My Mother, an "Emese aishes chayil" (Truly, a Woman of Valor)

When my mother made boiled chicken, it had to be really boiled, because the main thing was not the chicken but the chicken soup. So, she'd buy three or four pounds of eight or nine different soup greens for a penny or two and would put them into a large boiling pot with the chicken. It would boil for about ten hours so that, as she put it, "all the goodness of the greens went into the soup."

Of course, this was only in good times when some wonderful luck befell us. Otherwise, it was a bowl of potato soup at Ratner's Restaurant. But if there were some good times, if my mother got a job in a sweatshop sewing children's overalls or lady's rayon underwear (she was an expert on the zig-zag sewing machine), then she'd make nine or ten dollars a week, and she would make soup after she came back from a day of squinting over sewing.

The only way she could get me to eat the chicken is by buying sauerkraut, mustard, catsup, horseradish, Russian dressing, Italian dressing, French. . . . She had 17 spices out so I could dip the chicken into it and eat.

Raspberry Tea

4 tablespoons whole raspberry jam
4 teaspoons tea
4 tablespoons candle sugar (crystallized sugar)

Method for Candle Sugar: In a tall glass, dangle a string. Add sugar, then add hot water until glass is three-quarters full. Add enough sugar to supersaturate water. As it cools, sugar crystals will form around the string. Lift out "wick." Place spoon in glass (to prevent glass from breaking) and add hot tea, 1 tablespoon raspberry jam and 1 tablespoon candle sugar for each glass of tea.

RHODA MORGENSTERN/Kahlua Ice Cream Special

Rhoda

My name is Rhoda Morgenstern. I was born in the Bronx, N.Y., in December, 1941. I've always felt responsible for World War II.

The first thing I remember liking that liked me back was food.

I had a bad puberty; it lasted seventeen years.

I'm a high school graduate. I went to art school. My entrance exam was on a book of matches.

I decided to move out of the house when I was 24. My mother still refers to this as the time I ran away from home.

Eventually I ran to Minneapolis where it's cold and I figured I'd keep better. Now I'm back in Manhattan. New York, this is your last chance.

Kahlua Ice Cream Special   • Serves 3

Any fresh, fragrant fruit—peaches, apricots, nectarines, etc., peeled and sliced.
1 pint ice cream, vanilla or coffee
¼ cup Kahlua
Semi-sweet chocolate

Method: Combine vanilla or coffee ice cream thoroughly with Kahlua. Use about ¼ cup Kahlua to 1 pint ice cream, but let your own taste dictate the amount. If firmer consistency is desired, put mixture back into freezer until proper hardness is reached. Place freshly sliced fruit into pretty serving dishes and top with a generous dollop of the Kahlua ice cream. A scraping of semi-sweet chocolate swirled atop is positively worth every additional calorie.

TONY RANDALL/Cherry Cheese Graham Cracker Pie

Wild Night in Tulsa

I grew up in Tulsa.

I can remember my grandmother making her own noodles. She would roll out the dough real flat and with a great big long knife, she would go dit-dit-dit-dit across the board and right across the fingernails. In ten seconds she made a million noodles. They were done that fast, and they were delicious.

I remember the time my grandmother was baking a cherry pie and she called me into the kitchen to show me a cherry she had cut open. There, snuggled around the pit, was a worm. I couldn't taste a cherry for another twenty years. Kosher or traif.

One winter my family decided that we wanted something other than water to drink with our meat meals. We agreed to have soda pop. Being a frugal family, we bough a bottle-capping machine and proceeded to make a whole cellarful of homemade root beer. We made it with yeast, capped it and then let it ferment in the bottle.

One morning about three, we heard an explosion. One of the bottles had exploded. Soon, all of the bottles followed suit. It sounded like the cannons going off in the recording of Tchaikovsky's *1812 Overture*.

We went back to drinking water—a quiet drink.

Cherry Cheese Graham Cracker Pie

• Serves 6

16-18 graham crackers
¼ cup sugar
¼ cup butter or margarine, softened
½ pound cottage cheese
½ pound cream cheese
1 teaspoon vanilla
2 eggs
¾ cup sugar
Glaze

Method: Crumble graham crackers very fine with a rolling pin (or use your electric food mill). Blend ¼ cup sugar, butter and graham cracker crumbs (use your fingers). Press crust into a 9-inch pie pan. Mix cheeses, vanilla, eggs and ¾ cup sugar. Pour into prepared graham cracker crust. Bake in a 350-degree oven 20 minutes (or until set). Remove from oven and cool slightly.

Glaze

1 #2 can sour pitted cherries canned in water
Few drops red food coloring

1 tablespoon cornstarch
3 tablespoons sugar (or more, to taste)

Method: Drain cherries, reserve liquid. Add a drop or two of red food coloring to cherries. Combine and arrange cherries on top of baked pie. Measure 1 tablespoon cornstarch into a small saucepan. Combine drained juice from cherries with cornstarch in pan. (Do this slowly at first to make a smooth paste.) Add sugar and a drop or two of red food coloring. Cook, stirring constantly, till sauce thickens and clears. Cool slightly and spoon sauce over cherries. Refrigerate and serve cold.

DINAH SHORE/Pecan Rum Cakes

Southern Comfort

These are something special! In the good old days in Winchester, Tennessee, when all mothers were plump and forced everybody to eat a little more, my mother used to serve, at her ladies' bridge club luncheons, her special chicken salad with piping hot homemade rolls—and then these—probably with homemade ice cream. Just a little something to keep body and soul together until the good ladies could go home to cook dinner.

Pecan Rum Cakes

2½ cups sifted cake flour
1½ cups sugar
1 teaspoon salt
3½ teaspoons baking powder
½ cup softened butter, margarine or shortening
¾ cup milk
1½ teaspoons vanilla

4 egg whites (let egg whites warm to room temperature)
½ teaspoon rum extract
¼ cup rum
Icing (recipe below)

Method: Preheat oven to 350 degrees. Sift flour, sugar, salt and baking powder into large bowl of mixer. Add butter or shortening, milk and vanilla. Beat on slow speed until blended. Then beat at medium speed 2 minutes, occasionally scraping sides of bowl with rubber scraper. Add unbeaten egg whites, rum extract and rum. Beat 2 minutes longer at medium speed. Pour batter into one long 13 x 9 x 2½-inch pan (or two 8-inch pans) that you have greased, floured and lined with wax paper. Bake 35 to 40 minutes or until surface springs back when gently pressed with fingertips. Let cake cool and prepare icing.

Icing

½ **cup butter (1 stick)**
¾ **pound confectioners' sugar, sifted (scant 3 cups)**
   Salt
4 **tablespoons milk**
1½ **teaspoons vanilla**
   Rum
   Finely chopped pecans

Method: Cream butter and sugar with hand beater until fluffy. Add salt and stir in milk. Keep beating until very fluffy. Add vanilla. Cut cake into 1½-inch squares. Pour a generous teaspoon of rum on each cake square. Spread icing on all sides and roll in chopped fresh pecans. The icing part is pretty messy, but it all comes out beautifully as you roll it around in the chopped nuts. I use a chopping bowl for this. You can substitute moist coconut for nuts and you have Snow Rum Balls instead of Pecan Rum Cakes. Or, if you leave out the rum, you have plain Snow Balls, which are great too. Make them 2½ inches square and you have a dessert dish instead of an accompaniment. Makes about 44 little cakes.

This recipe is from *Someone's in the Kitchen with Dinah* (Doubleday).

ELKE SOMMER/German Coffee Cake

The Fifth Question
by Joe Hyams

Elke never had kosher food until I took her to a seder at my friend, Marshall Flaum's house. Not wanting to embarrass Elke, Marshall and I decided to read the service in English so she could follow along.

Elke didnt say anything. We read the Hagaddah in our native tongue and when we came to the traditional blessings, we were careful to point to the transliteration. When we came to the four questions, we honored Elke by asking her to read them. She rose regally, turned the transliterated part over and set her sights on the

Hebrew. As I was about to caution her that she was looking at the wrong page, she began, "Ma Nishtana Halailah Hazeh, Mikol Halelot. . . .'

Marshall and I sat flabbergasted as she read the Hebrew flawlessly.

Marshall recovered his composure first, "How, where?" He hadn't recovered that well.

"My father was a minister. He studied the Old Testament in its original. He taught me how to read Hebrew."

"But," I interrupted, "you never told me you knew how to read Hebrew."

Elke looked at me with her soulful and tantalizing eyes, "You never asked," she said simply, as she sat and began reading the answers for the four questions in Hebrew.

German Coffee Cake   • Serves 8

3 cups flour
5 teaspoons baking powder
1 teaspoon salt
¼ teaspoon nutmeg
¼ teaspoon cinnamon
¾ cup sugar
¼ cup vegetable shortening
2 eggs
1 cup milk

Method: Sift together flour, baking powder, salt, spices and sugar. Work vegetable shortening into dry ingredients. Add eggs combined with milk. Stir until smooth. Pour into a greased shallow pan (8 x 12). With fork, blend the first five ingredients below and spread smoothly on top of batter; then sprinkle with nuts:

¼ cup vegetable shortening
1 cup brown sugar
1/8 teaspoon salt
¼ cup flour
½ teaspoon cinnamon
1 cup coarsely chopped nuts

Bake in 350-degree oven 30 minutes.

MARK SPITZ/Carrot Ring

Jumping the Gun

My grandmother, who lived in Modesto, California, made wonderful little butternut cookies that required a great deal of time in the preparation. She also made delicious apricot turnovers. A portion to her was a nibble to me.

During the Olympics in Munich, I always ate the same thing for breakfast. It never varied. One morning I walked into the cafeteria and before I could pick out my usual breakfast, the dining room staff gave me a tray they had already prepared. The only drawback was that I usually ate eggs and hot cereal but by the time I got their prepared tray, everything was ice cold. I didn't have the heart to return it as the waiters were beaming because of their own thoughtfulness. After all, we were supposed to be ambassadors too.

Carrot Ring

1½ cups butter (¾ pound), at room temperature
1 cup brown sugar, firmly packed
4 eggs, separated

3 cups raw carrots, finely grated (approximately 1 pound)
2 tablespoons cold water
2 tablespoons lemon juice
2 cups flour
1 teaspoon baking soda
2 teaspoons baking powder
1 teaspoon salt
¼ cup bread crumbs

(Use 3-quart ring mold, lightly greased.)

Method: In electric mixer, cream butter with brown sugar, add egg yolks and beat until thick. Add grated carrots, water, lemon juice, flour, baking soda, baking powder and salt. Mix well on low speed. In separate bowl, beat egg whites until stiff. Fold beaten egg whites into carrot mixture. Dust greased ring mold with bread crumbs. Place carrot mixture in mold. Bake in pre-heated 350-degree oven 1 hour. Remove from oven and allow to cool 3 minutes. With dull knife, loosen edges and center of ring. Turn upside down on plate. Serve cold.

MEL TORME/Yellow Cake with Chocolate Icing

The Chocoholic Kid

I grew up in Chicago. On Friday nights at my grandmother's we would have the traditional Eve of Sabbath dinner. After the meal, those of us who were still able got up and went to the back porch. My uncles Art and Al, my dad and I, sang songs in harmony to work off our meals. The songs weren't the traditional Sabbath songs but World War I tunes. I played the uke, one of my uncles the clarinet, and we sang in three-part harmony. So, oddly enough, my grandmother's dinners were primarily responsible for the creation of the "Mel-Tones."

I was a radio personality at the age of eight. My mother would stand in the control booth and watch my performance. If she thought it was good, I was rewarded by a chocolate shake or a piece of cake— chocolate of course. At a very tender age I was hooked. I became a chocoholic.

Even now after a really good show, I find myself ordering a chocolate shake or malt or cake.

Yellow Cake with Chocolate Icing

• Serves 4-6

1 box yellow cake mix: Make as directed except add 1 egg and use whole milk in place of water

Icing

**3-ounce package cream cheese
2 or 3 tablespoons sour cream, at room temperature
1 teaspoon vanilla
4 squares semi-sweet chocolate
1 square unsweetened chocolate melted over double boiler and cooled to room temperature
2 or 3 cups powdered sugar**

Method: Melt 4 squares semi-sweet chocolate and 3 squares unsweetened chocolate over a double boiler. Allow chocolate to cool at room temperature. Combine cream cheese, sour cream and vanilla. Add cooled, melted chocolate. Add powdered sugar till desired consistency is reached. Spread over top and sides of cake.

ELI WALLACH/Non-dairy Date and Nut Bread

"My Cup Runneth Under"

We had a candy store in Little Italy in Brooklyn. At one seder a long time ago (so long ago that there were only three questions), we rigged a glass with a hollow tube with wine and left it for the mysterious stranger. When we began reading, the cup of wine started to diminish. However, it was too early in the seder for anyone to notice.

When the ten plagues came around, the level started to become more noticeable. By Dayenu, a few people realized what was happening and began to snicker. At meal time the glass was way below its original level. My parents glanced at each other and smiled. When the time came to open the door and let the mysterious stranger in, the wine had all but vanished. Since nobody said anything about it, I didn't know if the others thought I had perpetrated the gag or if they believed it was truly a miracle. After the seder, I no longer had to wonder. I was suitably punished.

Non-dairy Date and Nut Bread

1 teaspoon baking soda
1 cup boiling water
1 pound dates, cut
1 egg, separated
¼ cup sugar
¼ teaspoon salt
1 cup walnuts, chopped
1¾ cups all-purpose flour
1 teaspoon vanilla
Rind of 1 orange, grated

Method: Mix baking soda with water, pour over dates and let stand 10 minutes. Beat egg yolk, sugar and salt thoroughly. To this, add date mixture and chopped nuts. Add flour, vanilla, orange rind and then fold in beaten egg white. Spoon into greased 8 x 3½-inch pan. Bake 1 hour in 325-degree oven.

GENE WILDER/Mock Strudel

Child Prodigy

When I was seven years old I had a passion for strudel that exceeded my interest in most other things in life. It wasn't all strudel I loved—only my Bubby's and her cousin's (both ladies came over from Russia in 1911). On one particular day I went to visit my grandmother hoping to slip off to the strudel jar while I pretended to have to go to the bathroom, but to my surprise my grandmother was in the process of making a fresh batch.

I pulled up a stool and watched her as she finished rolling the dough. I saw her throw in a variety of goodies and then carefully roll everything up into one long tube. Then she took a long knife and sliced the tube at a very precise angle—which I remembered exactly—and put the ingredients onto a greased pan and then into the oven. I saw her set the dial at 350.

An hour later, I came busting into my own mother's kitchen, crying "Manma! Mama! I know how to make strudel."

"What are you talking about?" she said.

"I can make strudel," I answered very confidently.

"How do you do it?" she asked.

"Simple," I said. "First throw in all those things into the dough, then you roll it around just like this"—and I made circles with my extended arms—"then you take a seven-inch butcher's knife and cut the dough at this angle"—I showed her exactly which angle I meant—"and then you put it in the oven at 350."

This is the first time I have ever given away my Bubby's secret. I hope you will all enjoy it.

Ingredietns: (1) All those things you throw in. (2) Dough. (3) 7-inch butcher's knife. (4) A big pan. (5) An oven.

Mock Strudel

For those who don't have the time and patience to prepare traditional strudel, here is a simplified version:

½ pound butter
2 tablespoons sugar
2 eggs
¼ pint sour cream
2¼ cups all-purpose flour

Filling:

Jam
Dates, chopped
Nuts, chopped
Raisins (whole)
Turkish Delight, chopped (optional)
Shredded sweetened coconut (optional)

Method: Cream butter, add sugar, eggs and sour cream. Mix well. Add flour and chill dough in refrigerator overnight. Divide dough in three parts. Roll out each part about ¼-inch thick on a lightly floured board. Spread each part with jam, dates, nuts and raisins. Coconut or Turkish Delight may be added for variety. Roll like jelly rolls and bake in 350-degree oven 45 minutes to 1 hour. Cut in 1-inch slices while warm.

CELEBRITY INDEX

Henderson, Florence, 131
Hiller, Arthur, 95
Holtzman, Ken, 2
Hyams, Joe, 139

Jaffe, Sam, 96
Javits, Jacob, 113
Jessel, George, 3
Johnson, Arte, 97

Kaye, Danny, 76
Kaye, Stubby, 42
Kahn, Madeline, 132
Klein, Robert, 98
Klugman, Jack, 99
Koch, Howard, 77
Korman, Harvey, 78
Kruschen, Jack, 5

Lane, Abbe, 44
Lee, Michele, 100
LeRoy, Mervyn, 45
Lewis, Jerry, 133

Lewis, Robert Q., 46
Lewis, Shari, 47
Linden, Hal, 114

Macy, Bill, 14
Martin, Ross, 115
Matthau, Walter, 101, 134
Mererdith, Morley, 80
Merrill, Robert, 48
Morgenstern, Rhoda, 135
Morton, Gary, 30
Murray, Jan, 49

Newman, Barry, 65
Nidetch, Jean, 50, 116
Nimoy, Leonard, 6
Nye, Louis, 51

Persoff, Nehemiah, 102
Peters, Roberta, 66
Prelutsky, Burt, 23

Randall, Tony, 136

RECIPE INDEX

Coffee-toffee pie, 129
Cold schav (sorrel), 130
Cole slaw, 27
Collard, 92
Cookies, foot, 132
Crazy chicken, 76
Cucumber vichyssoise, 17

Date and nut bread, non-dairy, 143
Duckling, plum, 77
Dutch pea soup and meatballs, 12

Eggplant, Roumanian, 7
Essig fleish with prunes and apricots (sweet and sour
    ragout), 62

Farfel soup, Puerto Rican, 13
Fiesta salad, 25
Fish:
    baked fillet of flounder, 69
    baked fillet of sole, Russian style, 65
    baked stuffed, 67
    molded fillets, 66

Fish soup, milchig, 15
Flemish chicken stew (waterzooi de poulet), 79
Flounder, baked fillet of, 69
Foot cookies, 132
Fresh fruit kuchen, 123

Gedempte fleish (beef pot roast), 34
Gefilte chicken (a la fish), 72
German coffee cake, 140
Gogl-mogl, 126
Goulash, 30
Greek olive and herring salad, 21
Greens, 92

Home brew, 127
Honey carrots, 94
Hungarian potatoes, 98

Ice cream special, kahlua, 135

Kahlua ice cream special, 135
Kasha, 101, 104
Kasha Varnishka, 99
Kekletten (beef patties), 45

Knishes, 86
Knishes, lazy cheese, 95
Kosher caviar, 3
Kreplach, 59

Lamb, roast leg of, 47
Lamb shanks, braised, 58
Latkes, cauliflower, 91
Latkes, cheese, 116
Lazy cheese knishes, 95
Lima beans, baked, with flanken, 33
Lime pie, lyrical, 120
Limko, 73

Martini tuna spaghetti, 70
Matzo brie, 110, 118
Matzo Kneidlach (Passover dumplings), 16
Matzo schalet, 109
Meat dish, sweet and sour, 44
Meatball ragout, 50
Milchig fish soup, 15
Mish mosh, 35
Mock strudel, 145
Mushrooms and potatoes, 103

Noodle pudding, 90, 105

Olive and herring salad, Greek, 21

Pea soup and meatballs, Dutch, 12
Pears and caviar, 26
Pecan rum cakes, 138
Peppers, sweet and sour stuffed, 56
Persimmon pudding, 122
Pickled herring, 6
Pie, cherry cheese graham cracker, 136
Pie, coffee-toffee, 129
Pie, lyrical lime, 120
Pirogen (verenikas), 88
Plum duckling, 77
Poor man's caviar, 5
Potatoes, Hungarian, 98
Potato soup (przepalanka)
Potboiler, 31
Pot roast, beef, 34
Przepalanka (potato soup), 10
Puerto Rican farfel soup, 13

Ragout, sweet and sour, 62